BAKING
with
Joanna

BAKING

with

Joanna

All the Fun of Specialty Baking With Step by Step Instructions

JOANNA DUELL

ISBN: 979-8-89316-599-9 - eBook

ISBN: 979-8-89316-580-7 - Paperback

ISBN: 979-8-89316-581-4 - Hardcover

Acknowledgments

I want to give a special thanks to my oldest brother, Keith Duell, for inspiring me to write this cookbook. Thank you for always supporting, encouraging, and celebrating with me. You are so special to me. I also want to thank my sister, Amy Ahlfield, for loving to bake with me when I was little. You made baking so fun and still do. To Amy's husband, Isaac Ahlfield, I love the way you inspire me to dig deeper and explore the intricacies of my baking. To my second brother, Cyrus Duell, it is so fun that you are always willing to try the bakes I make. To the four of you, I love you and can't wait for our next Annual Christmas Bake-Off. Thank you to my parents, Andrew and Dondi Duell, for never complaining about buying more ingredients. You guys have been the best, and I love you both. Finally, I would like to thank my friends at Sterling Foursquare Church for being part of my baking journey. You all have been so supportive and encouraging and made my baking journey fun.

Table of Contents

Introduction

When I was just seven years old, I discovered my love of baking and created my first recipe by grabbing all the ingredients that I thought would be in an oatmeal cookie and microwaved them together in a few little cookies. My parents were my willing taste testers and supported me no matter how bad those cookies tasted. As I got older, I knew I wanted to create my own recipes. It was over my spring break in 2020 that I officially created my first recipe: macarons! Over the next four years I would create over sixty recipes that I designed myself in the areas of breads, mousses, cakes, soufflés, pastries, fillings, and other desserts. I perfected each of these recipes so that they would have the ideal textures, flavors, and sweetnesses. I am so excited to share with you all the recipes I have created from croissants to cream puffs to biscotti cookies to lemon mousse. With detailed step-by-step instructions and pictures, I have designed this cookbook so anyone can successfully make and enjoy all these bakes. I can't wait for you to join me on this baking journey!

Breads

Soft Breadsticks

Ingredients:

3 c. bread flour
1 pkg instant yeast (7 grams)
1 tsp salt
2 Tbsp honey
1 c. milk
1/4 c. water
5 Tbsp butter, softened

BAKE 400°F

Knead: 8–10 minutes in a stand mixer

Rise #1: 45–55 minutes

Rise #2: 45 minutes

Bake: 15–17 minutes

Yield: 16 breadsticks

These breadsticks are soft and flavorful.

With short rises, these breadsticks are quick and easy to make.

Measure out into a stand mixer the flour, yeast, salt, honey, milk, and water. Using the dough hook attachment, mix until a dough forms. Once a dough forms, slowly add the butter in 1/2–Tbsp chunks. Put 1 cube in, and mix for a few moments for it to start incorporating before adding the next piece.

Continue kneading for 8–10 minutes until the bread passes the windowpane test. To do a windowpane test, take a small piece of dough in your fingers. While holding the dough up to the light, gently stretch the dough. If the dough tears before you can see the light through the dough, it is not ready. If you can stretch the dough and see light through it before it tears, then the dough is ready.

After you've finished kneading the dough, place it in a lightly oiled bowl and let it rise for 45–55 minutes until double in size.

When the dough has done its first rise, we are ready to shape the breadsticks. Knock down the dough by punching it and deflating it. Then take a small amount of dough, shape it into a breadstick around 1 inch wide and 5–6 inches long, and place each breadstick onto a baking sheet. The dough might be a bit tacky, but this is okay. These will rise a lot when we bake them, so space them 1 1/2–2 inches apart. You will need 2 baking sheets.

Now the breadsticks are ready for their second rise. Drape a light towel over the breadsticks, or for the best rise, put the baking sheet in a proofing bag. Let them rise for 45 minutes.

During this time, preheat the oven to 400°F. When the dough is done proofing, place the baking sheets in the oven, and bake 15–17 minutes until golden brown. Transfer to a cooling rack to cool.

Enjoy your soft breadsticks!

Successful windowpane test

Shaped breadsticks before their final rise

Shaped breadsticks after their final rise

Soda Bread

Ingredients:

40g plain white flour
120g whole wheat flour
60g oat flour
185ml buttermilk
30ml whole milk
1/2 tsp plus 1/8 tsp
baking soda
1/4 tsp salt

Special Equipment:
Scale

BAKE 375°F
Knead: none
Rest: 30 minutes
Bake: 27 minutes
Yield: 1 loaf (12 servings)
Soda bread pairs very well with soup or even a soufflé. The most important thing when making this loaf is scoring it deep enough. Soda bread is a very hardy bread.

Preheat the oven to 375°F.

Measure out all the ingredients into a bowl and mix together until combined.

Line a baking sheet with parchment paper. Shape the dough into a ball, and place it on the parchment-lined baking sheet. Flatten the ball slightly by lightly pressing the top of the loaf. In order for this incredibly dense loaf to bake, it needs deep, deep scores. Score the dough like a plus sign to the point that the 4 sections are almost completely separated but still attached to each other. This step is very important.

The dough can be baked now, but for a slightly more flavorful loaf and a slightly higher rise in the oven, let the dough rest for 30 minutes.

Bake for 27 minutes until the bottom edge of the bread has just slightly browned. An instant-read thermometer should read 190ºF.

Enjoy your soda bread!

Slightly flattened ball of dough

The deep scores

White Bread

Ingredients:

500g bread flour
5g instant yeast
10.5g salt
350ml water, divided
50ml vegetable oil

Special Equipment:
Scale

BAKE 430°F
DROP TEMP TO 380°F
Knead: 10 minutes in stand mixer
Rise #1: 2 hours
Rise #2: 1 hour
Bake: 30 minutes at 430°F
Bake: 15 minutes at 380°F
Steam: entire bake
Yield: 1 loaf
With its high level of hydration, this bread is incredibly flavorful.
Steam the oven while your bread bakes to create a nice crust.
Slice the top of the dough before baking it to ensure the bread rises without tearing in the oven.

Measure the flour into the bowl of a stand mixer fitted with a dough hook. Add in the yeast and salt but on separate sides of the bowl. If you let them touch at this stage, you will kill the yeast. Add 200ml of the water and all of the oil, and mix until combined. Then add the remaining 150ml of water and mix till combined.

Knead for 10 minutes in a stand mixer or for 16 minutes by hand. I highly recommend that you knead this dough in a mixer. It is very wet and difficult to handle, but this extra hydration makes for an extremely flavorful dough!

Once the dough has developed enough gluten to pass the windowpane test, it is ready for its first rise. To do a windowpane test, take a small piece of dough in your fingers. While holding the dough up to the light, gently stretch the dough. If the dough tears before you can see the light through the dough, it is not ready. If you can stretch the dough and see light through it before it tears, then the dough is ready.

Let the dough rise for 2 hours until it has doubled in size. Knock down the dough by punching it and deflating it to get rid of the air bubbles. Transfer the dough to a 5 × 9-inch metal loaf tin or a 4 × 8-inch silicone loaf tin. Drape a light towel over the bread, or for the best rise, place the tin in a proofing bag, and leave to rise for 1 hour.

While the bread is rising, preheat the oven to 430°F. While the oven is preheating, place a broiler pan filled with water in the oven to steam the oven.

When the bread is done proofing, slash the top with 3 lines to allow the bread to expand in the oven without tearing.

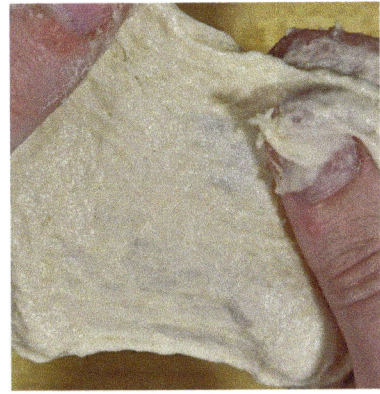

Successful windowpane test

Dough doubled in size after its first rise

Dough doubled in size after its second rise ready to bake

Bake the bread in the 430°F oven for 30 minutes. Then lower the temperature to 380°F (to prevent burning), and let it bake another 15 minutes. The bread is done when it is a dark golden brown or reads 190°F on an instant-read thermometer.

Remove the bread from the loaf tin immediately, and cool on a wire rack. It is best to let the bread cool down a bit before slicing and serving to allow the hot steam inside to cool.

Enjoy your white bread!

White bread when done baking

Blueberry Scones

Ingredients:

2 c. all-purpose flour
1/2 c. sugar
1/2 tsp salt
1/2 tsp baking soda
1 Tbsp baking powder
1/2 c. butter, chilled
1/4 c. whipping cream,
plus extra for brushing
1/4 c. buttermilk
1 egg
1 1/2 tsp vanilla
1 c. fresh blueberries

BAKE 400°F
Bake: 18 minutes
Yield: 8 scones
*Enjoy your scones warm
or cool.*
*Place your butter in the
freezer to make it easier to
grate.*
*Ensure you use fresh
blueberries when making
these scones.*

For this recipe, I recommend placing the chilled butter into the freezer for a few minutes so it will be easier to grate.

In a medium-sized bowl, combine the flour, sugar, salt, baking soda, and baking powder. Once the butter has sat in the freezer for a couple minutes, take it out and grate it into the flour mixture. I like to use a cheese grater to do this. Using a pastry cutter, cut the butter into the flour until it is pea-sized and the mixture has a crumbly texture. It is important not to overmix in this stage. Return the bowl to the freezer to keep cold while you do the next step.

In a small bowl, combine the whipping cream, buttermilk, egg, and vanilla, and whisk until the egg white is broken up and all ingredients are combined.

Take the flour mixture out of the freezer, and mix in the blueberries. It is very important to use fresh blueberries in this recipe. If you use frozen blueberries, the recipe will not work.

Add the wet ingredients to the flour mixture, and mix until the dough comes together. Turn the dough out onto the counter, and gently work it to mix in all the crumbs.

Form the dough into a 6-inch circle. The disk will be very thick. Using a dough scraper or a large knife, divide the dough into eighths.

Grated butter

The crumbly pea-sized mixture after cutting in the butter

The dough after mixing in the wet ingredients

Separate the triangles, and place them onto a parchment-lined baking sheet, spacing them at least 2 inches apart. After they have all been placed on the sheet, brush each scone with whipping cream, brushing the tops and sides.

Place the scones in the freezer while you preheat the oven to 400°F. As soon as the oven is hot, bake the scones for 18 minutes, until they are golden brown and a toothpick inserted into the middle comes out with only a few crumbles on it.

Enjoy your blueberry scones!

The thick 6-inch disk

The cut triangular scones brushed with whipping cream

Milk Bread

Ingredients:

Tangzhong:
2 Tbsp bread flour
1/2 c. milk

Dough:
3 Tbsp butter, melted
1/2 c. tepid milk
2 3/4 c. bread flour
1 tsp salt
1 pkg instant yeast (7 grams)
2 Tbsp sugar
1 egg
Tangzhong

BAKE 375°F
Knead: 8–10 minutes
Rise #1: 1 hour
Rise #2: 40 minutes
Bake: 32–34 minutes
Yield: 1 loaf
Milk bread makes excellent sandwich bread and is delightful when toasted. Milk bread is incredibly fluffy and light.

Egg wash:
1 egg yolk
1 Tbsp whipping cream

The first step in this recipe is to make the tangzhong on the stove. In a pot, over medium heat combine the 2 Tbsp of bread flour and 1/2 cup milk, and mix till combined and no lumps remain. Turn the heat to medium, and cook the mixture, whisking constantly until the mixture becomes very thick. If you do not whisk constantly, the mixture will not cook properly. Remove the tangzhong from the stove, and let cool a few moments in a separate bowl in the freezer or fridge. We want the mixture to cool until it is only warm.

Now it is time to make the dough. Melt the butter, and set aside to cool slightly. Warm the milk in the microwave. You want it to be warm not hot. If the temperature is much higher than 110°F, it will kill the yeast.

Add the bread flour, salt, yeast, and sugar into the bowl of a stand mixer, placing the salt, and yeast on separate sides of the bowl to ensure you don't kill the yeast. Add the melted butter, milk, egg, and the cooled tangzhong, and mix with a dough hook until combined. Continue kneading for about 8–10 minutes or until the dough passes the windowpane test (described below). When you finish kneading the dough, it will be soft and slightly sticky.

To do a windowpane test, take a small piece of dough in your fingers. While holding the dough up to the light, gently stretch the dough. If the dough tears before you can see the light through the dough, it is not ready. If you can stretch the dough and see light through it before it tears, then the dough is ready.

Now the dough is ready for its 1 hour rise. After an hour, once the dough has doubled in size, it is ready to be shaped.

Consistency of tangzhong when ready to take off the stove

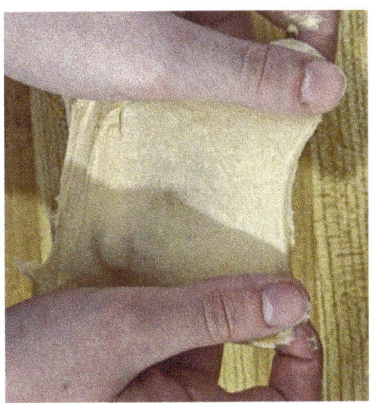

Successful windowpane test

Dough doubled in size after its first rise

Grease a 9 × 5-inch metal loaf tin with butter or shortening. Punch down the dough to knock the air out of it, then divide the dough into 3 sections. Taking 1 section at a time, form each section of dough into a ball. Place one of the dough balls on a floured counter and sprinkle the top with flour. Roll the dough into a roughly 12-inch long by 5-inch wide oval. The dough will be stretchy, but this is fine. Now we are going to fold the dough in thirds like a letter. Fold the top third of the dough over the middle of the dough. Then pull up the bottom third of the dough to also cover the middle.

Rotate the dough so that the fold line is vertical to you. Roll the dough out into a 12-inch long by 5-inch wide oval again. Now roll the dough up like a cinnamon roll so that the roll is 5 inches wide. Repeat this step with the other 2 balls of dough, and place each of the 3 sections into the loaf tin, spacing them evenly apart.

Let rise again for 40 minutes. To help the rise, I like to put the loaf tin in a proofing bag, but you can just lay a towel over the tin. You are looking for the dough to be around doubled in size and close to the rim of the tin.

Toward the end of this rise, preheat the oven to 375°F.

Once the dough has finished rising, brush the loaf with an egg wash. The egg wash I like to use is made of 1 egg yolk and 1 Tbsp of whipping cream. Brush the loaf with the egg wash, and bake for 32–34 minutes until it is golden brown and an instant-read thermometer reads 190°F.

Enjoy your milk bread!

One third of the dough rolled out to a 12-inch long by 5-inch wide oval

Oval folded in thirds and rotated 90 degrees

Milk bread before its final rise

Milk bread after its final rise and brushed with an egg wash

Focaccia

Ingredients:

Olive oil infusion:
1/2 c. olive oil
1 garlic clove, minced (1/2 tsp)
1 tsp dried thyme
1 tsp dried rosemary
1/4 tsp black pepper

Dough:
3 c. bread flour
2 tsp salt
1 pkg instant yeast (7 grams)
1 c. warm water
1/4 tsp honey
1/4 c. olive oil infusion
Lightweight toppings of choice

BAKE 450°F
Knead: using the stretch and fold method
Rise #1: 1 hour
Rise #2: 30–45 minutes
Bake: 15–20 minutes
Yield: 1 9 × 13-inch loaf
Focaccia is a delicious seasoned bread.
Pair with a pasta dish or a soup.
If you are making a half recipe use a 9-inch square dish or round pan.

Prebake topping:
1/4 c. olive oil infusion
1 garlic clove, minced (1/2 tsp)

The first step in this recipe is to infuse the olive oil with some spices to create a wonderful flavor for our bread. In a saucepan, combine 1/2 cup olive oil, minced garlic, thyme, rosemary, and black pepper. For the garlic, I like to use jarred minced garlic. Simmer the mixture over medium-low heat for 5–10 minutes until it smells aromatic. Set aside to cool to at least 110°F.

In a mixing bowl, combine the flour, salt, yeast, warm water, honey, and 1/4 cup of the olive oil infusion, saving the remaining 1/4 cup for later. The water should be between 100°F and 110°F—much hotter than this and you will kill the yeast. Mix until a dough forms, and leave it for its first rise.

After its first rise we need to strengthen the dough's gluten structure by using the stretch-and-fold method. To do this, pull up a corner of the dough, and fold it back over itself. Rotate the bowl a fifth turn and repeat. Do this 3 more times for a total of 5 stretch-and-folds.

After finishing the stretch-and-folds, place the focaccia dough into a 9 × 13-inch baking dish. Stretch the dough out to the sides of the dish as best you can. To help stretch the dough, I like to stretch it in the air like you would pizza dough before placing in the pan and stretching it to the sides. Allow to rise for 30–45 minutes until the dough has doubled in size.

Preheat the oven to 450°F.

Stretch-and-fold, part 1 – stretching up a corner of the dough

Stretch-and-fold, part 2 – folding the stretched corner back over the dough

Once the dough has done its short rise, poke the dough with your fingers to create the focaccia's iconic dimples. Then brush the top of the focaccia with the remaining 1/4 cup of the olive oil infusion and top with an additional minced garlic clove. Add any other lightweight toppings you'd like, such as sliced cherry tomatoes.

The bread is now ready to bake for 15–20 minutes until golden brown!

Enjoy your focaccia!

Focaccia dough stretched to the edges of the baking dish

Focaccia dough dimpled and and brushed with oil

Focaccia bread when done baking

Dutch Oven Bread

Ingredients:

360g bread flour
7g salt
4g instant yeast
252g water

Special Equipment:
Dutch oven
Scale

BAKE 450°F
Knead: none
Rise #1: 18 hours (in fridge)
Rise #2: 2–4 hours (on counter)
Bake: 15 minutes with lid and
20 minutes without lid
Yield: 1 loaf (8 servings)
*Dutch oven bread has a
wonderful crust that may even
crackle as it cools.*
*Dutch oven bread is very simple
and easy to make.*
*Because of its long rise in
the fridge, this bread is very
flavorful.*

Measure all the ingredients into a bowl, and mix until a dough forms. The dough may look very dry at first, but as you mix, the flour will absorb the water and form a slightly tacky dough. Put the bowl in the fridge, and leave to rise for 18 hours. This dough does not have to be kneaded, but it does still develop a gluten structure through what is called autolysis.

Autolysis is when gluten forms because the flour has had time to be fully saturated with the water and has self-aligned the protein molecules that make gluten strands. Normally we align these proteins ourselves through rigorously moving and shoving the dough during the kneading process, but this long rise eliminates the need for that.

After the dough has been in the fridge for 18 hours, take it out and knock down the dough by punching the air out of it. Form the dough into a circle loaf and place on a sheet of parchment paper. Let it sit on the counter and rise until double in size. This usually takes about 3 hours, but could take anywhere from 2 to 4 hours.

During this rise, place your Dutch oven into your cold oven and preheat the oven to 450°F. Allow the Dutch oven to sit in the fully hot oven for at least 30 minutes. This will get the Dutch oven to the same temperature as the actual oven.

After the 2–4 hour rise, use potholders to remove the Dutch oven from the oven, and carefully lower the loaf on the parchment paper into the Dutch oven.

Replace the lid, place the Dutch oven back into the oven, and let bake for 15 minutes with the lid on. Then remove the lid, and bake for another 20 minutes to allow for browning. The bread is done when it is golden brown and reads 190°F on an instant-read thermometer.

Enjoy your Dutch oven bread!

Bread dough before its rise on the counter

Bread dough doubled in size after its rise on the counter

Baguettes

Ingredients:

500g all-purpose flour
10g salt
3g instant yeast
325g water

Special Equipment:
Couche
Pizza peel (optional)
Pizza stone (or baking sheet)
Scale

PREHEAT 500°F
DROP TEMP TO 475°F: 15 MINUTES
DROP TEMP TO 450°F: 15 MINUTES
Knead: none
Rest #1: 15 minutes
Rise #1: 1 1/2 hours (on counter)
Rise #2: 18 hours (in fridge)
Rest #2: 30–45 minutes
Rise #3: 30–45 minutes
Bake: 15 minutes at 475°F
Bake: 15 minutes at 450°F
Yield: 3 baguettes
Baguettes are a crunchy bread that pairs well with many dishes including soufflés, soup, pasta, and more.
Buy a couche to rise your baguettes in and a pizza peel to help move the baguettes.

Measure the flour into a mixing bowl. Add the salt and the yeast, placing them on separate sides of the bowl to ensure you don't kill the yeast. Add the water and mix until a dough forms. Let rest on the counter for 15 minutes to relax the dough.

After the 15-minute rest, the dough is ready for its 1 1/2-hour rise on the counter. During this rise, the dough needs to have its gluten structure strengthened. We do this by using the stretch-and-fold method. We will do 3 stretch-and-fold sets during this 1 1/2-hour rise. Wet your hands, then grab a corner of the dough, stretch it up, and fold it back over the dough. Rotate the bowl a fifth turn and repeat. Do this 3 more times for a total of 5 stretch-and-folds. We will do 2 more sets of stretch-and-folds during this rise, spacing each set 30–45 minutes apart.

Once the rise is done, transfer the bowl to the fridge and allow the dough to rise for 18 hours.

After the 18-hour rise, remove the dough from the fridge and turn it out onto a floured counter. Gently roll the dough out into the shape of a rectangle roughly 9 by 13 inches. Now let the dough rest on the counter for 30–45 minutes, until the dough is a bit warmer. This will allow you to handle the dough more easily as you shape it without bursting all the air bubbles, which would result in a dense baguette.

Now it is time to shape the baguettes. First we need to set up our couche to ensure that when shaped, this wet dough does not spread during its final rise. First lightly spritz or brush your couche with water so that it is more pliable. With the couche flat, dust the entire couche with flour. This is important to prevent your dough from sticking to the couche. Next, pleat your couche so that there are long trenches to set the baguettes in once they are shaped.

Stretch-and-fold, part 1 – stretching up a corner of the dough

Stretch-and-fold, part 2 – folding the stretched corner back over the dough

The set up couche spritzed with water, dusted with flour, and pleated

Taking the baguette dough, divide the rectangle into 3 pieces, cutting along the width. Take 1 piece to shape into a baguette. Reflour the counter as needed to prevent the dough from sticking. Take your small rectangle with the short side parallel to you and fold the dough in thirds like you would a letter. Rotate the dough 90 degrees and repeat the letter fold.

Now, with the long side parallel to you, slightly lengthen and widen the rectangle gently into a 6-inch by 4-inch rectangle. Fold the top half of the dough toward the middle to meet it, but do not cover the middle. Seal the seam by pressing along the edge. Rotate the dough 180 degrees. Fold the top down toward the middle as well, and seal the seam again. The seams can overlap slightly, but not entirely.

Finally, with the long side still parallel to you, fold the baguette one last time. To do this, start from the right side of the baguette and use your left thumb as a guide to help you fold the dough in half. As you go along the baguette folding it in half, use your right palm to seal the dough using a gentle rolling motion along the seam as you are folding it in half along the length.

Using your hands, gently roll the baguette back and forth from the center to the edges, tapering the ends until you get a baguette that is about 12–13 inches long. Transfer the baguette to the couche, laying it seam side up in one of the trenches.

Repeat these steps for the other 2 baguettes.

Once all the baguettes have been placed in the couche, let them proof for 30–45 minutes until they have risen to about 1 1/2 times their size. When gently poked, they should spring back slowly.

The 6 by 4-inch rectangle

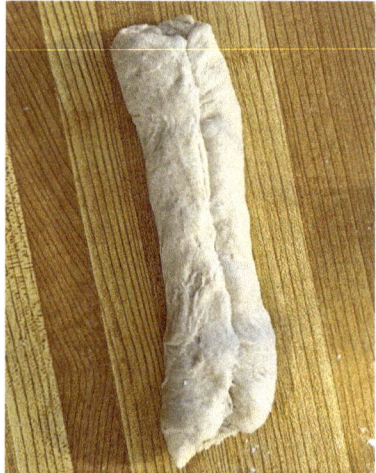

The 6 by 4-inch rectangle with its edges folded in towards the middle and the seam sealed

The final fold of the baguette using the left thumb as a guide

During this final rise, place the pizza stone and a broiler pan full of water into your oven and pre-heat to 500°F. If you do not have a pizza stone, use a regular baking sheet, but don't preheat it. The broiler pan should be as full of as much water as it can hold to ensure it doesn't run dry while the baguettes are baking. The steamed environment will give the baguettes a nice crust. Once the oven is hot, let the pizza stone and broiler pan of water sit in the oven for 15–30 minutes before baking the baguettes.

After the baguettes are finished with their final rise, we need to transfer them to the pizza stone. Carefully remove the hot pizza stone from the oven and set it on your stovetop or on a cooling rack.

Roll 1 of the baguettes off of the couche and onto a pizza peel. If you do not have a pizza peel, use a piece of parchment paper. Then roll the baguette off the pizza peel and onto the pizza stone aiming to have the seam side down. Use the pizza peel or your hands, to straighten the baguette once it is on the baking stone if it is crooked. Transfer the other 2 baguettes to the pizza stone if they fit. If you can only fit 2 baguettes on at a time, that is alright. Wait until the first 2 are done to bake the third.

Once the baguettes are on the pizza stone, it is time to slash them with a bread lame or a sharp knife. To slash with a bread lame, hold the lame at a 30 degree angle with the curve facing down. Using the sharp corner, use quick diagonal motions toward your body to slash the dough several times for the traditional look. Or you can do one large slash down the middle lengthwise. The baguettes are now ready to bake.

Put the baguettes into the oven and immediately reduce the temperature to 475°F. Bake the baguettes for 15 minutes at this temp. Then rotate the baking stone 180 degrees, reduce the temp to 450°F, and bake for another

The baguettes in the couche before their final rise

The baguettes one and a half times their size after their rise

The slashed baguettes on a pizza stone ready to bake

15 minutes until the baguettes are a deep golden brown.

Enjoy your baguettes!

Brioche Buns

Ingredients:

2 1/4 c. bread flour
3/4 tsp salt
5g instant yeast
1/4 c. milk
3 eggs plus 1 yolk
9 Tbsp butter, slightly softened
3 Tbsp sugar

Special Equipment:
Instant-read thermometer
Scale

PREHEAT 400°F
BAKE 350°F
Knead: 25–35 minutes
Rise #1: 4 hours (in fridge)
Rise #2: 1 1/2 hours (on counter)
Bake: 20 minutes at 350°F
Yield: 8 buns
Brioche is a fully enriched dough.
These brioche buns are light and fluffy.

Measure the flour into the bowl of a stand mixer with a dough hook attachment. Add in the salt and yeast but on separate sides of the bowl to ensure you don't kill the yeast. Add the milk and the eggs, and mix together until a dough starts to form and there is no unmoistened flour. The dough may look dry at first, but it will come together.

From here, knead the dough on medium speed for 3 minutes. Then let the dough rest for 3 minutes. Do this 3-minute, 3-minute process a few times until the dough starts to look smoother and can stretch a short amount.

These 3-minute periods of rest are important and help the dough not rise in temperature. Brioche dough has a hard time developing gluten, and the long, constant kneading raises the temp of the dough, which can make the butter in the dough melt. If the butter melts and separates, it will ruin the brioche. The goal is to not let the dough rise above 78°F, but I have had brioche rise to 79°F and turn out fine.

After this 3-minute, 3-minute process, start adding the butter. We will add the butter in 2 portions. The first portion will be a third of the butter. With the mixer running on medium speed, add 1 Tbsp of the butter. Wait until it is mostly incorporated before adding another.

Once all of the first portion of butter is incorporated, it is time to add the sugar. Mix in the sugar, and wait until it is fully incorporated to add the rest of the butter.

After the sugar is mixed in, keep adding the butter, 1 Tbsp at a time, waiting until each piece is mostly mixed in before adding the next piece.

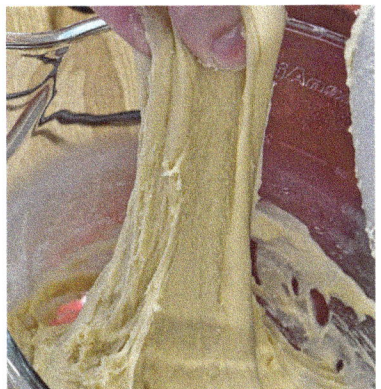

The stretch of the dough after the 3-minute, 3-minute process

The dough stretched into a long thin sheet after all kneading is finished

After all the butter is mixed into the dough, let the dough take a 3-minute rest. After this rest, continue kneading the dough on high speed, periodically checking that the temp is not above 78°F. Knead the dough until it does not stick to sides of the bowl much. When a portion of the dough is stretched into a long thin sheet, it should not rip. If the dough does get to 78°F before the kneading is finished, let the dough rest for another 3 minutes. Then resume kneading making sure the dough does not rise above 78°F.

After you're done kneading the dough, check the temperature. If the temp is 77°F or above, this is good. If the temp is below 77°F, the dough will need a short 1-hour rise before going into the fridge. We will do this short rise after we do our slap-and-folds.

The slap-and-fold method will make the dough less sticky and strengthen it. To do this, turn the dough out onto a clean unfloured counter. Pick up the left side of the dough, quickly lifting it up into the air, then swing the right side of the dough underneath, and slap it down onto the counter. Then fold the left side of dough, which is still in your hands, back over the dough. Repeat this motion several times until the dough loses its stickiness and becomes smooth.

At this point, if the dough was below 77°F it will need its 1-hour rise on the counter. Otherwise, skip this rise.

Now the dough is ready for its rise in the fridge to develop wonderful flavor. Place the dough in a greased bowl, and cover it with plastic wrap. Let rise for 4 hours.

After the dough has had its 4-hour rise in the fridge, line a baking sheet with parchment paper.

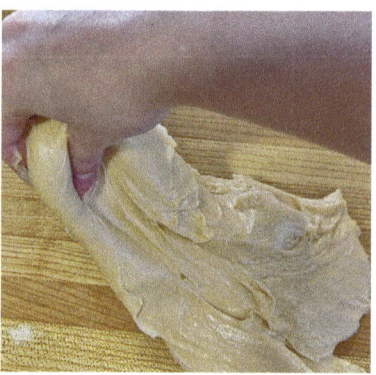

Slap-and-fold part 1 – picking up the left side of the dough

Slap-and-fold part 2 – swinging the right side of the dough underneath and slapping it down onto the counter

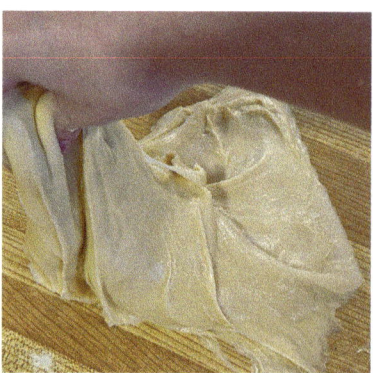

Slap-and-fold part 4 – repeat

Slap-and-fold part 3 – folding the dough in your hands back over itself

Turn the dough out onto a floured counter and divide the dough into 8 pieces. Then shape each piece into a ball. To form a ball, take 1 piece of dough into your hands. Gently pull the edges of the dough underneath while rotating the dough ball so that you get a smooth bun. Place the buns on the prepared baking sheet to rise.

Let the buns rise for 1 1/2 hours until they have about doubled in size. During this rise, preheat the oven to 400°F.

Now it is time to bake the buns. Place them in the oven, immediately reduce the oven temperature to 350°F, and bake them for 20 minutes until they are a deep golden brown.

Enjoy your brioche!

The buns before their rise

*The buns doubled in size
after their rise*

The buns when they are done baking

Cottage Loaf

Ingredients:

500g bread flour
10g salt
5g instant yeast
280g water
50g butter, softened

Special Equipment:
Scale

BAKE 450°F
DROP TEMP TO 375°F
Knead: 5–10 minutes
Rise #1: 1 hour
Rise #2: 1 hour
Bake: 15 minutes at 450°F
Bake: 20–25 minutes at 375°F
Yield: 1 loaf
A cottage loaf is a double stacked loaf.
A cottage loaf is soft and flavorful.

Measure all the ingredients into the bowl of a stand mixer, making sure to place the salt and yeast on separate sides of the bowl to ensure you do not kill the yeast. Mix the ingredients together until a dough forms. The dough may look a bit dry, but this is fine. Once the dough has formed, knead for about 5–10 minutes until it is smooth.

Place the dough into a bowl that has been lightly brushed with oil, and let rise for 1 hour, until the dough has doubled in size.

Once the dough has doubled, turn it out onto a lightly floured surface, and knock down the dough by punching the air out of it and deflating it.

After knocking down the dough, take a third of the dough and set it aside. Take the remaining dough and shape it into a circle loaf. To do this, flatten the dough a bit into a small, rough rectangle. With the short side parallel to you, roll the dough away from you into a log. Now with the long side of the log parallel to you, fold the left and right ends of the dough into the middle, and press them into the dough to seal them. You should have a square now.

Flip the dough over so that the seam is underneath, and take the dough into your hands. Now rotate the dough in your hands while gently pulling the sides of the dough underneath to turn the square into a circle with a taut surface. This process of shaping the loaf will ensure that it rises upward and not outward. Place this loaf onto a baking sheet lined with parchment paper. Then, repeat this process for the other third of the dough.

Once you have shaped the smaller loaf, place it on top of the bigger circle, making sure to center it.

Dough doubled in size after 1st rise

Two-thirds portion of dough flattened out into a small rough rectangle

Two-thirds portion of dough rectangle rolled up into a log

Now we need to fuse the 2 stacked loaves together. To do this, dip your middle and index fingers in flour. Using those 2 fingers, press through the top loaf and all the way through the bottom loaf until you can feel the pan underneath. Fusing the loaves together like this will ensure they rise and bake as 1 large loaf.

Drape a piece of plastic over the loaf and leave the dough for its second rise for 1 hour.

During this rise, preheat the oven to 450°F. After the dough has risen, it is time to slash the dough. We will slash the cottage loaf a total of 8 times, making 4 slashes on each side of the upper loaf and 4 slashes on each side of the bottom loaf.

Now the loaf is ready to bake! Bake the loaf for 15 minutes at the 450°F temperature. Then lower the temperature, and bake the loaf for another 20–25 minutes until it is golden brown and reads 190°F on an instant-read thermometer.

Enjoy your cottage loaf!

Left and right ends folded into the middle forming a square

One-third portion of dough flattened out into a small rough rectangle

One-third portion of dough rectangle rolled up into a log

1. Left and right ends folded into the middle forming a square

4. The fused loaves

2. Smaller loaf on top of the larger loaf

5. The loaf after its 2nd rise

3. Fusing the loaves together

6. The scored loaf

Hot Cross Buns

Ingredients:

Buns:
4 1/4 c. bread flour
1 tsp cinnamon
3/4 tsp allspice
1 tsp salt
2 pkg instant yeast (7 grams each)
1/2 c. sugar
4 Tbsp butter, softened
1 c. milk
2 eggs

Filling:
1 c. dried fruit, nuts, or chocolate pieces

BAKE 375°F
Knead: 8–12 minutes
Rise #1: 2 hours
Rise #2: 1 hour
Bake: 20 minutes
Yield: 12 buns
Hot cross buns are a spiced bun.
Have fun with the filling. Fill with any dried fruit, nuts, or chocolate you'd like.
Enjoy as a breakfast or pair with a soup.

Crosses:
3/4 c. bread flour
7 1/2 Tbsp milk
3/4 tsp vanilla

Into the bowl of a stand mixer that's been fitted with a dough hook, mix together the flour, cinnamon, allspice, salt, yeast, and sugar, making sure to add the salt and yeast on separate sides of the bowl to ensure you don't kill the yeast.

Add the butter, milk, and eggs to the bowl and mix the ingredients until a dough forms. We will add the dried fruit and nut filling in a later step. Continue kneading on medium speed for 8–12 minutes until the dough passes the windowpane test. To do a windowpane test, take a small piece of dough in your fingers. While holding the dough up to the light, gently stretch the dough. If the dough tears before you can see the light through the dough, it is not ready. If you can stretch the dough and see light through it before it tears, then the dough is ready.

Let the dough rise for 1 1/2–2 hours until double in size.

Once risen, turn the dough out onto a lightly floured counter, and roll out into a rectangle measuring roughly 9 by 12 inches. Sprinkle the filling evenly over the rectangle. Roll up the dough so that you have a 12-inch-wide log. Then twist the log into a circle so that it is one large spiral. Gently knead or press the dough together so that it becomes one lump of dough again. This process will make sure that the filling is evenly distributed.

Separate the dough into 12 even pieces, and shape each one into a ball. To shape the balls, take a piece of dough into your hands. Gently pull the edges of the dough underneath while rotating the dough ball so that you get a smooth bun. If using fruit as your filling, make sure no pieces of fruit are showing. If there are pieces of fruit showing, they will burn in the oven. Repeat this shaping step with the other 11 pieces of dough, placing each on a parchment-lined baking sheet.

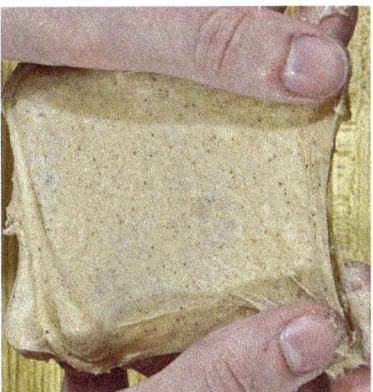

Successful windowpane test

The dough doubled in size after its first rise

The dough returned to one lump after adding the fruit

Let the buns rise for 1 hour until they have a little less than doubled in size, around a 75 percent increase in size. While they are rising, preheat the oven to 375°F.

Once the buns have finished rising, it is time to pipe the crosses.

In a small bowl, mix together the flour, milk, and vanilla until a semi-thick paste forms and there are no clumps of flour. Transfer the mixture to a piping bag or a plastic zipper bag, snip off a 1/8 inch nozzle, and pipe crosses onto the buns. Now they are ready to bake!

Bake for 20 minutes until the buns are golden brown and an instant-read thermometer reads 190°F.

Enjoy your hot cross buns!

The buns a little less than doubled in size after their second rise

The prepared cross topping

The buns when done baking

Crosses piped on the buns

Concha Pan Dulce

Ingredients:

Dough:
4 c. all-purpose flour
1 pkg instant yeast (7 grams)
1 tsp salt
1/2 c. sugar
3/4 c. half-and-half
1/2 c. butter, melted
1 tsp vanilla
3 eggs

Topping:
1 c. powdered sugar
1 c. flour
1 tsp vanilla
1/2 c. butter, softened

BAKE 350°F
Knead: 8–12 minutes
Rise #1: 2 hours
Rise #2: 1–2 hours
Bake: 18 minutes
Yield: 12 buns
Enjoy conchas as a breakfast or as a dessert.
Dye the topping any color you'd like.
Add a little cocoa powder as you are mixing together the topping to give it a chocolate flavor.

Into the bowl of a stand mixer that's been fitted with a dough hook, add the flour, yeast, salt, sugar, half-and-half, butter, vanilla, and eggs, making sure to add the salt and yeast on separate sides of the bowl to ensure you do not kill the yeast. Mix until a dough forms. Continue kneading for 8–12 minutes until the dough is smooth, soft, and has some stretch to it.

Transfer the dough to a lightly oiled bowl, and let rise for 2 hours until the dough is doubled in size.

When there is about 20–30 minutes left on the rise, make the topping. Mix together with a spatula the powdered sugar, flour, vanilla, and butter until a dough forms.

If you would like, this is the point where you can divide the topping to dye it different colors. (To make chocolate conchas, mix a little cocoa powder into the topping.) Ultimately, we will divide the topping into 12 even pieces to go on top of our 12 concha buns.

Once the concha dough has finished rising, turn it out onto a floured counter, and knock it down by punching the air out of it and deflating it. Separate the dough into 12 even pieces. Shape the dough pieces into balls by taking them into your hands and gently pulling the edges of the dough underneath while rotating the dough ball so that you get a smooth bun, then place them on baking sheets.

Take a piece of the topping, and flatten it with your palms until it is a disk thin enough to cover the entire concha bun but does not touch the pan. Place the disk onto a bun, then repeat with the other 11.

Prepared topping ready to use or to dye a color

Now it is time to carve a design onto the concha buns. Using a knife, score the topping in the pattern of your choice. A shell is the traditional pattern for conchas. When you score, only score the depth of the topping. You do not want to cut the actual bun underneath.

Once you have finished the designs on the conchas, leave them for their second rise for 1–2 hours. We are looking for them to rise to about 1 1/2 times their original size. As they rise, the designs will start to stretch out. Preheat the oven to 350°F when the second rise is almost finished.

After their second rise, the conchas are ready to bake! Bake them for 18 minutes until the bottoms of the buns are golden brown or an instant-read thermometer reads 190°F.

Enjoy your concha pan dulce!

Concha buns before their rise

Concha buns one and a half times their size after their rise

Cinnamon Rolls

Ingredients:

Cinnamon rolls:
4 1/4 c. bread flour
1 tsp salt
2 pkg instant yeast (7 grams each)
1/2 c. sugar
4 Tbsp butter, softened
1 c. milk
2 eggs

Cinnamon filling:
8 Tbsp butter, softened
1 1/2 Tbsp cinnamon
2/3 c. dark brown sugar

BAKE 350°F
Knead: 8–10 minutes in a stand mixer
Rise #1: 4 hours (in fridge)
Rise #2: 45 minutes–1 hour and 15 minutes (on counter)
Bake: 24–26 minutes
Yield: 12 cinnamon rolls
These cinnamon rolls are light, fluffy, and flavorful. They have a perfect brown sugar-cinnamon filling.

Frosting:
1 oz. cream cheese
4 Tbsp butter, softened
1 c. powdered sugar
1 tsp vanilla
4 tsp whipping cream

Measure out into a stand mixer bowl that's been fitted with a dough hook the flour, salt, yeast, sugar, butter, milk, and eggs, making sure to add the salt and yeast on separate sides of the bowl to ensure you don't kill the yeast. Knead the dough in the mixer for 8–10 minutes until the dough passes the windowpane test. To do a windowpane test, take a small piece of dough in your fingers. While holding the dough up to the light, gently stretch the dough. If the dough tears before you can see the light through the dough, it is not ready. If you can stretch the dough and see light through it before it tears, then the dough is ready.

Once you've finished kneading the dough, transfer it to a greased bowl, and place it in the fridge to rest for 4 hours.

Once the dough is done resting in the fridge, turn it out onto a heavily floured counter. Roll the dough out into a 12 by 18-inch rectangle. If you are making a half recipe, your rectangle should be 12 by 9 inches. Flour the top of the dough as needed to prevent the rolling pin from sticking and lift the dough periodically to prevent it from sticking to the counter.

Once the dough is rolled out, we are ready to add the cinnamon filling. Spread the softened butter over the entire surface of the dough leaving a 1/4- to 1/2-inch border. In a bowl, mix together the cinnamon and brown sugar. Sprinkle the mixture over the dough, and spread around evenly. Gently press the brown sugar mixture into the butter to make it stick.

Now we are ready to roll up the dough. Taking the long side of the dough, roll up the dough along the 12-inch side to form an 18-inch long log. Trim the ends to make them even. Cut the log into 12 cinnamon rolls, and place them into a greased 9 × 13-inch glass baking dish.

Cover the cinnamon rolls lightly and let proof for 45 minutes to 1 hour and 15 minutes, until

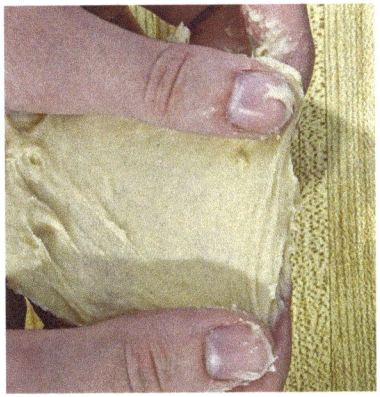
Successful windowpane test

Butter spread on the dough

Cinnamon brown sugar mixture spread over butter

doubled in size. When you near the end of the proofing time, preheat your oven to 350°F.

Once the cinnamon rolls are done rising, place them in the oven, and bake for 24–26 minutes, until they are golden brown. As soon as you take the cinnamon rolls out of the oven make the frosting.

To make the frosting, cream together the cream cheese and softened butter. Add the powdered sugar and beat together. Add the vanilla and whipping cream, and continue mixing until a frosting forms.

Spread the frosting onto the cinnamon rolls and serve.

Enjoy your cinnamon rolls!

Cinnamon rolls before their rise

Cinnamon rolls doubled in size after their rise

Finished frosting ready to use

Cinnamon rolls when done baking

Mousses

Chocolate Mousse

Ingredients:

2.8 oz. semisweet baking chocolate (56% cacao)
4 oz. whipping cream
2 oz. egg whites (about 2 eggs)
2.8 oz. corn syrup

Special Equipment:
Scale
Instant-read thermometer

Yield: 4 servings
The cooled chocolate must be between 90°F and 100°F to incorporate properly.
Enjoy this mousse as a standalone dessert or as a filling for another dessert.

First, we need to melt the chocolate. Add the chocolate to a medium-sized heat-safe bowl. Melt the chocolate in 15–20 second increments in the microwave, stirring in between each burst. When using the microwave, it is important to make sure to not overheat the chocolate or it will seize up, and you will need new chocolate. Take the chocolate out of the microwave when there are only a few small pieces of chocolate left unmelted. The residual heat will melt them.

Mostly melted chocolate with only a few unmelted pieces

Set the chocolate aside to cool slightly while you prepare the other ingredients. The chocolate needs to be between 90°F and 100°F when we mix everything together. If the chocolate is cooler than this, it will harden when you mix everything together, leaving you with a grainy mousse. If it is hotter than this, it will melt the whipped cream.

Next, let's make the whipped cream. Whip the cream until it is the consistency of whipped cream and is spreadable. It should be soft but still relatively firm.

Egg whites whipped to soft peaks

Now it is time to whip up the egg whites. Whip the egg whites on medium speed until they reach soft peaks. You will know you have reached soft peaks when you can pick up the beaters and the peaks of the egg whites bend over.

Once you have reached soft peaks, add the corn syrup in 3 additions, adding a third at a time and whipping in between each addition. When you add the corn syrup, drizzle rather than pour it over the egg whites.

Egg whites whipped to stiff peaks

Once you have added all the corn syrup, continue whipping the egg whites on high speed until they reach stiff peaks. You will know you have reached stiff peaks when you can pick up the beaters and the peaks of egg whites stand straight.

Once the chocolate has cooled to between 90° and 100°F, we are ready to fold in the egg whites. Add the egg whites in 2 portions. Fold in a third of the egg whites until mostly combined, then fold in the remainder.

Finally, fold in the whipped cream all at once. Once it is fully mixed in, the mousse is finished!

You can enjoy the mousse immediately, but it's preferable to let it fully set up in the fridge for 15–20 minutes. If you would like your mousse cold when you serve it, let it sit in the fridge for an hour.

Enjoy your chocolate mousse!

Raspberry Mousse

Ingredients:

10 oz. raspberries
1/2 tsp vanilla
5 oz. whipping cream
1 oz. egg whites
4 oz. corn syrup

Special Equipment:
Scale
Instant-read
thermometer

Yield: 4 servings
Strain out the seeds for a
smooth mousse.
Enjoy this mousse as a
standalone dessert or as a
filling for another dessert.

First, we need to make a raspberry compote. Place the raspberries into a medium-sized sauce-pan along with the vanilla and 1 Tbsp of water. Turn the heat to medium-high. Once the mixture starts simmering, continue cooking the berries for 26–30 minutes, stirring often. Cook the raspberries until they have released their juices and the sauce has thickened some.

Transfer the compote to a food processor or a blender, and blend the mixture to create a smooth sauce. Then strain the compote through a fine strainer to remove the seeds. Place the compote in the freezer to cool down to 100°F while you prepare the other ingredients.

Next, let's make the whipped cream. In a medium-sized bowl, whip the cream until it is the consistency of whipped cream and is spreadable. It should be soft but still relatively firm.

Now it is time to whip up the egg whites. Whip the egg whites on medium speed until they reach soft peaks. You will know you have reached soft peaks when you can pick up the beaters and the peaks of egg whites bend over.

Once you have reached soft peaks, add the corn syrup in 5 additions, whipping in between each addition. When you add the corn syrup, drizzle rather than pour it over the egg whites.

Once you have added all the corn syrup, continue whipping the egg whites on high speed until they reach stiff peaks. You will know you have reached stiff peaks when you can pick up the beaters and the peaks of egg whites stand straight.

Once the compote has cooled to at least 100°F, we can fold it into the whipped cream. Pour the compote over the whipped cream, and fold them together until combined.

Finally, add the egg whites and fold until smooth. The mousse is now ready to serve.

Consistency of raspberry compote when ready to take off the stove

Egg whites whipped to soft peaks

Egg whites whipped to stiff peaks

If you would like to serve the mousse cold, place the mousse in the fridge for 45 minutes.

Enjoy your raspberry mousse!

Strawberry Mousse

Ingredients:

9 oz. strawberries
1/2 tsp vanilla
5 oz. whipping cream
1 oz. egg whites
4 oz. corn syrup

Special Equipment:
Scale
Instant-read
thermometer

Yield: 4 servings
Strain out the seeds for a smooth mousse
Feel free to whip in additional corn syrup if the finished mousse is not sweet enough.
Enjoy this mousse as a standalone dessert or as a filling for another dessert.

First, we need to make a strawberry compote. Cut the tops off the strawberries and halve them. Place them in a medium-sized saucepan along with the vanilla and 1 Tbsp of water. Turn the heat to medium-high. Once the mixture starts simmering, continue cooking the berries for 18 minutes, stirring often. Cook the strawberries until they have released their juices, are soft, and the sauce has thickened some.

Transfer the compote to a food processor or a blender, and blend the mixture to create a smooth sauce. Then strain the compote through a fine strainer to remove the seeds. Place the compote in the freezer to cool down to 100°F while you prepare the other ingredients.

Next, let's make the whipped cream. In a medium-sized bowl, whip the cream until it is the consistency of whipped cream and is spreadable. It should be soft but still relatively firm.

Now it is time to whip up the egg whites. Whip the egg whites on medium speed until they reach soft peaks. You will know you have reached soft peaks when you can pick up the beaters and the peaks of egg whites bend over.

Once you have reached soft peaks, add the corn syrup in 5 additions, whipping in between each addition. When you add the corn syrup, drizzle rather than pour it over the egg whites.

Once you have added all the corn syrup, continue whipping the egg whites on high speed until they reach stiff peaks. You will know you have reached stiff peaks when you can pick up the beaters and the peaks of egg whites stand straight.

Once the compote has cooled to at least 100°F, we can fold it into the whipped cream. Pour the compote over the whipped cream, and fold them together until combined.

Consistency of strawberry compote when ready to take off the stove

Egg whites whipped to soft peaks

Egg whites whipped to stiff peaks

Finally, add the egg whites and fold until smooth. The mousse is now ready to serve.

If you would like to serve the mousse cold, place the mousse in the fridge for 45 minutes.

Enjoy your strawberry mousse!

Blueberry Mousse

Ingredients:

8 oz. blueberries
1/2 Tbsp lemon juice
3 Tbsp sugar
1 tsp vanilla
5 oz. whipping cream
1 oz. egg whites

Special Equipment:
Scale
Instant-read
thermometer

Yield: 4 servings
Strain out the seeds for a
smooth mousse.
This mousse has a wonderful
purple color.
This mousse needs to sit
in the fridge for at least 45
minutes to set up.
Enjoy this mousse as a
standalone dessert or as a
filling for another dessert.

First, we need to make a blueberry compote. Place the fresh blueberries into a small or medium-sized saucepan. Add the lemon juice, sugar, vanilla, and 1 Tbsp of water. Turn the heat to medium-high. Once the mixture starts simmering, continue cooking the blueberries for 18 minutes, stirring occasionally, until they have released their juices and the sauce has thickened.

Consistency of blueberry compote when ready to take off the stove

Take the blueberry compote off of the stove, and transfer it to a food processor or a blender. Blend the compote until it is completely smooth, then strain it through a fine strainer to remove the seeds. Place the compote in the freezer to cool it down to 100°F while you prepare the rest of the ingredients.

Next, in a medium-sized bowl, whip the cream until it is the consistency of whipped cream and is spreadable. It should be soft but still relatively firm.

Egg whites whipped to soft peaks

Next, let's whip the egg whites in a small bowl. On medium speed, whip the egg whites until they are white and foamy. Then increase the speed to high, and continue to whip them until you reach stiff peaks. You will know you have reached stiff peaks when you can pick up the beaters and the peaks of egg whites stand straight.

Once the blueberry compote has cooled to at least 100°F, pour it over the whipped cream and fold to combine. Once combined, add the whipped egg whites and fold to incorporate.

Egg whites whipped to stiff peaks

Transfer the mousse to the fridge, and allow to sit for 45 minutes to an hour to fully develop its flavor.

Enjoy your blueberry mousse!

Blackberry Mousse

Ingredients:

12 oz. blackberries
1/2 Tbsp lemon juice
3 Tbsp sugar
2 tsp vanilla
5 oz. whipping cream
1 oz. egg whites

Special Equipment:
Scale
Instant-read
thermometer

Yield: 4 servings
Strain out the seeds for a smooth mousse.
This mousse has a wonderful burgundy color.
Enjoy this mousse as a standalone dessert or as a filling for another dessert.

First, let's make a blackberry compote. Place the fresh blackberries into a small or medium-sized saucepan. Add the lemon juice, sugar, vanilla, and 1 Tbsp of water. Turn the heat to medium-high. Once the mixture starts simmering, continue cooking the blackberries over medium heat for 18 minutes until they have released their juices and the sauce has thickened.

Take the blackberry compote off of the stove, and transfer it to a food processor or a blender. Blend the compote until it is completely smooth. Then strain it through a fine strainer to remove the seeds. Place the compote in the freezer to cool it down to 100°F while you prepare the rest of the ingredients.

Next, in a medium-sized bowl, whip the cream until it is the consistency of whipped cream and is spreadable. It should be soft but still relatively firm.

Next, let's whip the egg whites in a small bowl. On medium speed, whip the egg whites until they are white and foamy. Then increase the speed to high, and continue to whip them until you reach stiff peaks. You will know you have reached stiff peaks when you can pick up the beaters and the peaks of egg whites stand straight.

Once the blackberry compote has cooled to at least 100°F, pour it over the whipped cream and fold to combine. Once combined, add the whipped egg whites and fold to incorporate.

The mousse is now ready. If you would like to serve your mousse cold, place it in the fridge for an hour.

Enjoy your blackberry mousse!

Consistency of blackberry compote when ready to take off the stove

Egg whites whipped to stiff peaks

Lemon Mousse

Ingredients:

2 Tbsp lemon juice
0.6 oz. white chocolate
6 oz. whipping cream
1/2 tsp vanilla
1.2 oz. egg whites
1.8 oz. sugar

Special Equipment:
Scale

Yield: 4 servings
By adding the lemon juice to the egg whites, we create a silky mousse.
Enjoy this mousse as a standalone dessert or as a filling for another dessert.

First, juice a lemon, strain out the pulp, and set the juice aside.

In a very small bowl, melt the white chocolate in the microwave in 10–15 second bursts, taking care to notice when the chocolate is mostly melted. When the chocolate is mostly melted, stop microwaving it, and let the residual heat finish melting the chocolate as you stir. Set aside.

Egg whites whipped to soft peaks

In a medium-sized bowl, weigh out the whipping cream and add the vanilla. Whip the cream until it is thicker but not the consistency of whipped cream yet. Add the melted white chocolate and continue whipping until the cream is spreadable and is the consistency of whipped cream.

Next, in a small bowl, measure out the egg whites. Whip the egg whites on medium speed until they reach soft peaks. You will know you have reached soft peaks when you can pick the beaters up and the peaks of egg whites bend over.

Consistency of the egg whites after adding the sugar and beating until it starts to whip up

Once you reach this stage, with the mixer running, add the sugar in a steady stream. Alternatively, add the sugar in 3 additions, mixing in between each addition. Once all the sugar is added, continue mixing on high speed until the mixture whips up again to a consistency close to soft peaks. You will not reach soft peaks this time.

Add the lemon juice to the whipped egg whites, and whip them together until the lemon juice is incorporated and the mixture holds stiff peaks.

Egg whites whipped to stiff peaks after adding the lemon juice

Fold the egg whites into the whipped cream, and the lemon mousse is finished!

Enjoy your lemon mousse!

Cakes

Vanilla Cake

Ingredients:

4 c. all-purpose flour
3 tsp baking powder
1/4 tsp salt
11 Tbsp butter, softened
2 c. sugar
4 egg yolks
3 tsp vanilla
2/3 c. milk
1 c. half-and-half
1 1/2 tsp lemon juice

BAKE 350°F

Bake: 38–41 minutes

Yield: 2 9-inch cakes

This cake recipe was designed to be great for carving.

This cake is delicious and melt-in-the-mouth.

The lemon juice adds a nice touch of flavor.

Heating up the milk strengthens its properties and produces a moist, soft, and strong cake.

Preheat your oven to 350°F.

Measure out into a medium-sized bowl the flour, baking powder, and salt. Mix them together and set aside.

In the bowl of a stand mixer that's been fitted with a whisk attachment, cream the softened butter for 30 seconds. Scrape down the sides of the bowl and add the sugar. Whip until the mixture is light and fluffy. This will take about 1–2 minutes.

Butter and sugar beaten until light and fluffy

Add in the 4 egg yolks and the vanilla, and mix for 1 minute.

In a saucepan on the stove, warm the milk over medium heat, stirring frequently. Milk burns easily, so do not go above medium heat, and make sure you are stirring frequently. Heat the milk until the little bubbles in the milk line the edge of the pan. This will happen right before the milk starts to simmer. Take the milk off the stove.

Little bubbles in the milk lining the edge of the pan

While the mixer is running on low speed, pour half of the milk into the butter mixture. Once that portion of milk has mixed in, add half of the dry ingredients. Add the rest of the milk, and mix until combined. Then add the rest of the flour, and mix until combined.

Finally, add the half-and-half and the lemon juice, and mix until combined.

Finished cake batter ready to bake

Grease and flour 2 9-inch round pans.

Divide the batter evenly between the pans, and bake the cake for 38–41 minutes, until a toothpick inserted into the center comes out with only a few crumbs on it.

Transfer the cake pans to a cooling rack for 10 minutes, then remove the cakes from their tins.

Enjoy your vanilla cake!

Cake when done baking

Flourless Chocolate Torte Cake

Ingredients:

13.6 oz. semisweet baking chocolate (56% cacao)
9 Tbsp butter
3/4 tsp vanilla
1 1/2 tsp instant coffee
1/4 plus 1/8 tsp baking powder
3 Tbsp warm milk
3 eggs
7 1/2 Tbsp sugar
Whipped cream, for garnish

BAKE 350°F

Bake: 19 minutes

Yield: 12–16 servings

This torte cake is rich and flavorful.

This is a lovely torte cake that has a similar texture to ganache.

It is crucial to mix in the baking powder before you mix in the milk.

Special Equipment:
Scale (optional)

Preheat the oven to 350°F.

First, let's melt the chocolate and butter. Place them in a bowl, and put the bowl over a pot of water that is 1 inch deep. Make sure the water is low enough that the bottom of the bowl does not touch the water. Turn the heat to medium-high. Stir occasionally until the chocolate and butter have melted. Set the bowl aside on a pot holder or a cooling rack, and mix in the vanilla.

Next, dissolve the instant coffee in 3/4 tsp water and add it to the chocolate mixture.

Then mix in the baking powder. It is crucial that the baking powder is mixed into the chocolate mixture BEFORE we add the milk; otherwise, the milk will take on a sour flavor when it mixes with the acidic chocolate and coffee. The baking powder neutralizes this acidity.

Next, mix in the warm milk. The milk must be warm so it doesn't harden the chocolate mixture.

Now let's beat together the eggs and sugar. Place the eggs and sugar in a mixing bowl, and beat them on medium speed until they look frothy and have lots of air.

Finally, whisk the egg mixture into the chocolate mixture.

Flour and grease a 9-inch round cake pan. Then pour the batter into the prepared pan. Bake the torte for 19 minutes, until the edges are set and the middle jiggles slightly when you wiggle the pan.

Let the torte cool on a cooling rack, then remove the tin.

Garnish with whipped cream.

Enjoy your flourless chocolate torte cake!

The frothy eggs and sugar after beating

The finished chocolate torte batter in its pan

Chocolate torte cake when done baking

Fluffy Honey Vanilla Cake

Ingredients:

24 Tbsp butter
1 1/4 c. sugar
4 eggs
2 Tbsp vanilla
4 c. flour
1 tsp baking powder
1/2 tsp salt
1 1/4 c. milk
1 c. honey

Special Equipment:
12 mini Bundt pans

BAKE 325°F
Bake: 28–30 minutes
Yield: 12 mini Bundt cakes
This cake pairs nicely with a lemon drizzle.
This cake has a fluffy, melt-in-the-mouth texture unlike anything I've had before.

Preheat the oven to 325°F, and prepare your mini Bundt pans by greasing and flouring them. I have found that using a pastry brush to grease the Bundt molds helps to make sure they get greased everywhere.

Measure out the butter into a large mixing bowl. Beat with an electric mixer for 2 minutes to cream the butter. Add the sugar, and beat until light and fluffy.

Add 2 of the eggs, and continue mixing until they are combined. Add the other 2 eggs, and continue to mix until combined. Next, add the vanilla. As the vanilla is mixing in, the mixture may look curdled, but this is fine.

In a separate medium-sized mixing bowl, combine the flour, baking powder, and salt. Then pour half of the flour mixture into the butter mixture. Once combined, add the milk and mix. Then beat in the rest of the flour.

Once all the flour is mixed in, add the honey and mix until combined. When you are finished mixing, do a few spatula folds to ensure that all the batter is thoroughly mixed.

Divide the batter between the 12 Bundt molds. Bake in the oven for 28–30 minutes, until a toothpick inserted into the cake comes out with only a few crumbs on it.

Take the cakes out of the oven, and let them sit for 5 minutes. Then turn them out of their molds. They should pop right out.

Serve plain or with a lemon drizzle.

Enjoy your fluffy honey vanilla cakes!

Butter and sugar beaten until light and fluffy

Finished batter

Cakes removed from their molds after baking

Tres Leches Cake

Ingredients:

Cake batter:
1 c. all-purpose flour
1 1/2 tsp baking powder
1/4 tsp salt
4 eggs, separated
3/4 c. sugar, divided
1/3 c. milk
1 1/2 tsp vanilla

Milk syrup:
14 oz. evaporated milk
10 oz. sweetened condensed
 milk
1/3 c. whipping cream

BAKE 350°F
Bake: 14 minutes in 2
9-inch round pans or 14–19
minutes in a 9 × 13-inch
baking dish
*This cake is wonderfully
light and bright.*
*Make this cake in 2 round
pans or in a rectangular
baking dish.*

**Whipped cream
topping:**
2 c. whipping cream
3 Tbsp sugar

Special Equipment:
Scale

In a small bowl, combine the flour, baking powder, and salt. Set aside.

Take your 4 eggs and separate them, putting the yolks into a medium bowl and the whites into another medium bowl.

Add 1/2 cup of the sugar to the yolks, and beat on high speed until the yolks are thick and a pale yellow. Mix in the milk and the vanilla.

Now turn your attention to beating the egg whites. With the mixer on medium speed, beat the egg whites until they reach soft peaks. You will know you have reached soft peaks when you can pick the beaters up and the peaks of egg whites bend over.

Once you reach this stage, with the mixer running add the remaining 1/4 cup sugar in a steady stream, or add the sugar in 2 portions, mixing between each addition. Once all the sugar is added, continue mixing on high speed until you reach stiff peaks. You will know you have reached stiff peaks when you can pick the beaters up and the peaks of egg whites stand straight. Set aside.

Now take the flour mixture, and fold it into the egg yolk mixture. Once they are combined, fold a third of the egg whites into the batter until mostly incorporated. Then fold in the remainder of the egg whites.

Grease either 2 9-inch round pans or a 9 × 13-inch baking dish. Pour the batter into your prepared pan(s). If you are baking 2 9-inch round pans, bake for 14 minutes. If baking in a 9 × 13-inch baking dish, bake for 14–19 minutes. The cake is done baking when a toothpick inserted into the center comes out clean.

Allow the cake to fully cool. Once it's cool, prick the entire surface of the cake with a fork.

Egg yolks and sugar beaten until thick and a pale yellow

Egg whites whipped to soft peaks

Egg whites whipped to stiff peaks

In a medium-sized bowl, combine the evaporated milk, sweetened condensed milk, and whipping cream. Once combined, pour the milk syrup over the cake.

Next, let's make the whipped cream topping. Whip the cream with the sugar until it reaches the consistency of whipped cream. Spread the whipped cream over the cake.

Enjoy your tres leches cake!

Surface of the cake pricked with a fork

Milk syrup poured over the cake

Chocolate Lava Cake

Ingredients:

6 oz. semisweet baking
chocolate (56% cacao)
8 Tbsp butter, plus
extra for preparing the
ramekins
2 whole eggs
2 egg yolks
1/4 c. plus 2 Tbsp sugar
1/8 tsp salt
1 tsp vanilla
1/4 c. cocoa powder plus
extra for dusting the
ramekins

BAKE 450°F

Bake: 6–9 minutes

Yield: 6 lava cakes

*Lava cakes should be enjoyed
soon after removing from the
ramekins.*

*Chocolate lava cakes are
delicious paired with ice cream.
Thoroughly buttering and
dusting the ramekins is
extremely important.
Dust the ramekins with either
flour or cocoa powder.*

Special Equipment:
4-oz. ramekins (6 count)

Preheat the oven to 450°F.

First, we need to prepare the ramekins. Brush each of the ramekins with softened butter, making sure to coat all the corners and ridges. Butter all the way to the rim of the ramekins. Using a pastry brush will make this easier. Next, place a small amount of flour or cocoa powder into each of the ramekins. Tap the flour or cocoa powder around the bottom and sides of the ramekins, making sure to coat the entire ramekin. Dump out the excess flour or cocoa powder. Transfer the ramekins to a baking sheet.

Now onto preparing the lava cakes! Place the chocolate and butter in a bowl, and put the bowl over a pot of water that is 1 inch deep. Make sure the water is low enough that the bottom of the bowl does not touch the water. Turn the heat to medium-high. Stir occasionally until the chocolate and butter have melted. Set aside.

In a medium-sized bowl, beat the whole eggs, yolks, sugar, salt, and vanilla on high speed until the mixture is thick and a pale yellow.

Pour the chocolate mixture over the egg mixture. Sprinkle the cocoa powder into the bowl, and fold everything together until it is combined.

Pour the batter evenly into the 6 ramekins and bake 6–9 minutes, until the edges of the cakes are set but the middle is still wobbly.

Take the lava cakes out of the oven, and allow to cool for 1 minute. Next, to remove the lava cakes from their ramekins, place a small plate over the top of the ramekin. Using a pot holder that has grips to help you hold onto the ramekin, flip the plate right side up, and set it on the counter. Allow the upside-down ramekin to sit for 10 seconds, then lightly tap the top and edges of the ramekin with a spoon to release the lava cake.

Mixture beaten until thick and a pale yellow

Lava cake batter portioned into ramekins

Lava cakes when done baking

Gently lift the ramekin up off the plate. The lava cake should be released. If not, tap the ramekin again, and gently shake it side to side to release the lava cake.

Add vanilla ice cream if desired.

Enjoy your chocolate lava cakes!

Coffee Cake

Ingredients:

Streusel topping:
1/2 c. brown sugar
1/4 c. flour
1 1/2 tsp cinnamon
3 Tbsp butter, softened

Batter:
1 1/2 c. all-purpose flour
1 tsp baking powder
1/4 tsp baking soda
8 Tbsp butter, softened
3/4 c. sugar
2 eggs
1 tsp vanilla
1/3 c. buttermilk

BAKE 350°F
Bake: 40 minutes
Yield: 9 × 9 inch square dish
Make sure the streusel
topping is fine and crumbly.
This coffee cake is delicious
served warm.
Half the streusel goes in the
middle of the coffee cake and
half goes on top.

Preheat the oven to 350°F.

First, we need to make the streusel topping. In a medium-sized bowl, mix together the brown sugar, flour, and cinnamon. Next, cut in the softened butter using a fork or pastry cutter until the mixture is fine and crumbly.

Next, let's start on the batter. In a medium-sized bowl, combine the flour, baking powder, and baking soda.

In another medium-sized bowl, cream the softened butter for 30 seconds. Add the sugar, and beat until the mixture is light and airy.

Add the eggs, vanilla, and buttermilk to the butter mixture, and mix until combined. Then add the flour mixture, and mix until combined.

Grease a 9 × 9-inch square baking dish, and pour half of the batter into the pan. Evenly spread half of the streusel topping over the batter. Pour the other half of the batter into the pan, and sprinkle the rest of the streusel on top of the batter.

Bake the coffee cake for 40 minutes, until a toothpick inserted into the center comes out with only a few crumbs on it.

Enjoy your coffee cake!

Finished streusel topping

Butter and sugar beaten until light and airy

Finished batter

Layered coffee cake ready to bake

Devil's Food Cake

Ingredients:

2 oz. semisweet baking chocolate (56% cacao)

1/2 c. cocoa powder

1/2 c. water

1/2 Tbsp instant coffee

7 Tbsp butter

1 c. sugar

2 eggs

1/2 tsp vanilla

1/4 c. buttermilk

1/4 c. sour cream

1 1/8 c. all-purpose flour

1 tsp baking soda

1/4 tsp salt

BAKE 350°F

Bake: 22–26 minutes

Yield: 2 9-inch cakes

It is important to sift the flour as you add it to the batter in this recipe. Make sure you bake this batter as soon as you make it.

Preheat the oven to 350°F, and prepare two 9-inch cake pans by greasing and flouring them.

The first step in this recipe is to create a sauce that we will mix with our batter. Into a saucepan, place the chocolate, cocoa powder, water, and instant coffee. Over medium heat, while stirring constantly, whisk the mixture until it starts to bubble. Take it off the stove, and transfer it to another dish. Place plastic wrap over the surface area of the chocolate sauce, and leave it to cool in the freezer while we make the batter.

Completed chocolate sauce

Place the butter into a stand mixer bowl or a medium-sized bowl. Beat on medium speed for 30 seconds to cream the butter. Then add the sugar, and beat until light and fluffy.

Add the 2 eggs and the vanilla, and beat until combined. Add the buttermilk and the sour cream, and continue to beat until combined. Next, add the chocolate sauce to the batter, and mix to combine.

In a separate bowl combine the flour, baking soda, and salt. Once combined, sift the flour into the chocolate batter, and mix until combined.

Butter and sugar beaten until light and fluffy

IMMEDIATELY divide the batter evenly into your prepared pans. Bake for 22–26 minutes, until a toothpick inserted into the center comes out with only a few crumbs on it.

Allow the cakes to cool on a cooling rack before frosting.

Frost with my chocolate frosting recipe or another frosting of your choice.

Enjoy your devil's food cake!

The cakes when done baking in the oven

Soufflés

Vanilla Soufflés

Ingredients:

4 Tbsp unsalted butter
5 Tbsp all-purpose flour
1 1/3 c. milk
1 vanilla bean (optional)
4 egg yolks
2 tsp vanilla
1/4 tsp salt
6 egg whites
1/4 tsp cream of tartar
6 Tbsp sugar

Ramekins:

2 Tbsp butter, softened
8 tsp sugar

PREHEAT 425°F
BAKE 375°F
Bake: 16–19 minutes
Yield: 8 individual soufflés
Make sure you enjoy your soufflés moments after they come out of the oven. Soufflés are eaten in their ramekins.
Bake a soufflé for 16–17 minutes for a wetter center and 18–19 minutes for a drier center.

Special Equipment:
8-oz. ramekins (8 count)

Preheat your oven to 425°F.

First, we need to prepare the ramekins. Divide the 2 Tbsp of softened butter between the 8 ramekins. Using a pastry brush, butter the bottoms and sides of the ramekins, making sure to coat all the corners and ridges. Butter all the way to the rim of the ramekins using upward strokes to help the soufflés rise in the oven.

Next, place 1 tsp of sugar in each of the ramekins. Coat the entire ramekin with the sugar, making sure to cover all the butter by tapping and turning the ramekin. Dump out the excess sugar. Place the ramekins on a baking sheet. There should be at least an inch of space between the ramekins to help with airflow in the oven.

Now let's make the soufflés! First, we need to make a simple white sauce on the stove. To do this, place your butter in a skillet and melt it over medium heat.

Once melted, add the flour. Stirring constantly, cook the flour until it no longer smells like raw flour and looks very bubbly. While whisking, add the milk. Continue whisking until the sauce becomes very thick, much thicker than a typical white sauce. Transfer the white sauce to another bowl, and allow to cool slightly.

If you would like to use a vanilla bean, prepare it now. Cut it into 2 halves along the length. In one motion, slide the knife down each bean half, scraping out the tiny vanilla beans. Add these tiny beans to the white sauce.

Next, separate the 6 eggs. Add only 4 of the egg yolks directly to the white sauce along with the vanilla and salt. Whisk together to combine. Discard the excess 2 yolks.

Place the 6 egg whites in a large bowl. Add the cream of tartar, and whip the egg whites on medium speed until they reach soft peaks. You will know you have reached soft peaks

Prepared ramekin

Consistency of white sauce when ready to take off the stove

Egg whites whipped to soft peaks

when you can pick the beaters up and the peaks of egg whites bend over.

Once you reach this stage, with the mixer running, add the sugar in a steady stream, or add the sugar in 3 portions, mixing in between each addition. Once all the sugar is added, continue mixing on high speed until you reach stiff peaks. You will know you have reached stiff peaks when you can pick the beaters up and the peaks of egg whites stand straight.

Fold a third of the egg whites into your white sauce mixture until mostly incorporated. Then fold in the remainder of the egg whites.

Once fully combined, divide the soufflé batter between the 8 ramekins. I like to use a very large serving spoon to do this.

Place the baking sheet in the 425°F oven, and IMMEDIATELY decrease the oven temp to 375°F. Bake the soufflés for 16–19 minutes, until they are well risen, the edges are set, and the center wobbles ever so slightly. Avoid opening the oven door while the soufflés are baking so that you do not collapse them. The only thing that can collapse a soufflé is a rapid drop in temperature, which is why they deflate soon after they come out of the oven.

A soufflé baked for 16–17 minutes will have more of a wobble and be more saucy on the inside. A soufflé baked for 18–19 minutes will have less of a wobble and be firmer on the inside. You can choose your preference and adjust the bake time accordingly.

As soon as the soufflés come out of the oven, they need to be eaten. They will deflate within a few minutes of being taken out of the oven.

Eat them right out of the ramekins with a spoon.

Enjoy your vanilla soufflés!

Egg whites whipped to stiff peaks

Portioned out soufflé batter

Lemon Soufflés

Ingredients:

8 egg yolks
1 Tbsp lemon zest
4 Tbsp all-purpose flour
4 Tbsp sugar
1 c. half-and-half
2 Tbsp butter
1/2 c. lemon juice
10 egg whites
1/8 tsp cream of tartar
1/2 c. sugar

Ramekins:

2 Tbsp butter, softened
8 tsp sugar

PREHEAT 425°F
BAKE 375°F
Bake: 16–17 minutes
Yield: 8 individual soufflés
Make sure you enjoy your
soufflés moments after they
come out of the oven.
Soufflés are eaten in their
ramekins.
These lemon soufflés are
wonderfully silky and light.

Special Equipment:
8-oz. ramekins (8 count)

Preheat your oven to 425°F.

First, we need to prepare the ramekins. Divide the 2 Tbsp of softened butter between the 8 ramekins. Using a pastry brush, butter the bottoms and sides of the ramekins, making sure to coat all the corners and ridges. Butter all the way to the rim of the ramekins using upward strokes to help the soufflés rise in the oven.

Prepared ramekin

Next, place 1 tsp of sugar in each of the ramekins. Coat the entire ramekin with the sugar, making sure to cover all the butter by tapping and turning the ramekin. Dump out the excess sugar. Place the ramekins on a baking sheet. There should be at least an inch of space between the ramekins to help with airflow in the oven.

Now let's make the soufflés! First we need to make a crème pâtissière (pastry cream) on the stove to be the base of our soufflés.

Separate your 10 eggs. Place 8 of the egg yolks in a medium-sized saucepan and 10 egg whites into a large mixing bowl. Discard the excess 2 yolks.

Next, zest and juice the lemons and set the juice aside. Into the 8 egg yolks, add the zest, flour, sugar, and half-and-half. Mix until combined.

While whisking constantly, heat the mixture over medium heat until it has thickened and is bubbling big bubbles. Once it starts bubbling big bubbles, continue to whisk constantly, and cook the crème pâtissière for another minute. This ensures that the mixture will thicken when cooled.

Take the pastry cream off the heat, and press it through a fine sifter to remove any bits of cooked egg. Then add the butter, and whisk until incorporated. Next, add the lemon juice, and stir to combine.

Now it is time to whip the egg whites. Add the cream of tartar, and whip the egg whites on medium speed until they reach soft peaks. You will know you have reached soft peaks when you can pick the beaters up and the peaks of egg whites bend over.

Once you reach this stage, with the mixer running, add the sugar in a steady stream, or add in 3 portions, mixing in between each addition. Once all the sugar is added, continue whipping on high speed until you reach stiff peaks. You will know you have reached stiff peaks when you pick up the beaters and the peaks of egg whites stand straight.

Fold the egg whites into the pastry cream a third at a time. Add the next third once the current third is mostly incorporated. As soon as you finish folding in the egg whites, it is important to immediately bake the soufflés.

Divide the soufflé batter evenly between the 8 ramekins. You will fill the ramekins all the way to the brim. I like to use a very large serving spoon to divide the batter.

Place the baking sheet in the 425°F oven, and IMMEDIATELY decrease the oven temp to 375°F. Bake the soufflés for 16–17 minutes, until they are well risen and slightly browned. Avoid opening the oven door while the soufflés are baking so that you do not collapse them. The only thing that can collapse a soufflé is a rapid drop in temperature, which is why they deflate soon after they come out of the oven.

As soon as the soufflés come out of the oven they need to be eaten. They will deflate within a few minutes of being taken out of the oven.

Eat them right out of the ramekins with a spoon.

Enjoy your lemon soufflés!

Egg whites whipped to soft peaks

Egg whites whipped to stiff peaks

Chocolate Soufflés

Ingredients:

8 oz. semisweet baking chocolate (56% cacao)
1/2 c. half-and-half
6 egg yolks
2 tsp vanilla
1/4 tsp salt
6 egg whites
1/8 tsp cream of tartar
6 Tbsp sugar

Ramekins:

2 Tbsp butter, softened
8 tsp sugar

PREHEAT 425°F
BAKE 375°F
Bake: 16–17 minutes
Yield: 8 individual soufflés
Make sure you enjoy your soufflés moments after they come out of the oven.
Soufflés are eaten in their ramekins.
Bake a soufflé for 16 minutes for a saucier center and 17 minutes for a firmer center.

Special Equipment:
8-oz. ramekins (8 count)

Preheat your oven to 425°F.

First, we need to prepare the ramekins. Divide the 2 Tbsp of softened butter between the 8 ramekins. Using a pastry brush, butter the bottoms and sides of the ramekins, making sure to coat all the corners and ridges. Butter all the way to the rim of the ramekins using upward strokes to help the soufflés rise in the oven.

Next, place 1 tsp of sugar in each of the ramekins. Coat the entire ramekin with the sugar, making sure to cover all the butter by tapping and turning the ramekin. Dump out the excess sugar. Place the ramekins on a baking sheet. There should be at least an inch of space between the ramekins to help with airflow in the oven.

Now let's make the soufflés! Place the chocolate and the half-and-half into a bowl, and put the bowl over a pot of water that is 1 inch deep. Make sure the water is low enough that the bottom of the bowl does not touch the water. Turn the heat to medium-high. Stir occasionally until the chocolate has melted and it has become a smooth mixture. Set the bowl aside on a pot holder or on a cooling rack.

Separate the 6 eggs, placing the whites in a medium-sized bowl and the yolks into the chocolate mixture. Along with the egg yolks, add the vanilla and salt to the chocolate mixture, and stir to combine.

Now turn your attention to the egg whites. Add the cream of tartar, and whip the egg whites on medium speed until they reach soft peaks. You will know you have reached soft peaks when you can pick the beaters up and the peaks of egg whites bend over.

Prepared ramekin

Egg whites whipped to soft peaks

Once you reach this stage, with the mixer running, add the sugar in a steady stream, or add in 3 portions, mixing in between each addition. Once all the sugar is added, continue mixing on high speed until you reach stiff peaks. You will know you have reached stiff peaks when you can pick the beaters up and the peaks of egg whites stand straight.

Fold a third of the egg whites into your chocolate mixture until mostly incorporated. Then fold in the remainder of the egg whites.

Once fully combined, divide the soufflé batter between the 8 ramekins. I like to use a very large serving spoon to do this.

Place the baking sheet in the 425°F oven, and IMMEDIATELY decrease the oven temp to 375°F. Bake the soufflés for 16–17 minutes, until they are well risen, the edges are set, and the center wobbles ever so slightly. Avoid opening the oven door while the soufflés are baking so that you do not collapse them. The only thing that can collapse a soufflé is a rapid drop in temperature, which is why they deflate soon after they come out of the oven.

A soufflé baked for 16 minutes will have more of a wobble and be more saucy on the inside. A soufflé baked for 17 minutes will have less of a wobble and be firmer on the inside. You can choose your preference on the bake.

As soon as the soufflés come out of the oven they need to be eaten. They will deflate within a few minutes of being taken out of the oven.

Eat them right out of the ramekins with a spoon.

Enjoy your chocolate soufflés!

Egg whites whipped to stiff peaks

Portioned out soufflé batter

Blackberry Soufflés

Ingredients:

16 oz. blackberries
1 tsp vanilla
6 Tbsp sugar
4 egg yolks
2 Tbsp all-purpose flour
1 c. half-and-half
2 Tbsp butter
6 egg whites
1/8 tsp cream of tartar

Ramekins:

2 Tbsp butter, softened
8 tsp sugar

PREHEAT 425°F
BAKE 375°F
Bake: 16–17 minutes
Yield: 8 individual soufflés
Make sure you enjoy your soufflés moments after they come out of the oven. Soufflés are eaten in their ramekins.
These blackberry soufflés have a beautiful purple color.

Special Equipment:
8-oz. ramekins (8 count)

Preheat your oven to 425°F.

First, we need to prepare the ramekins. Divide the 2 Tbsp of softened butter between the 8 ramekins. Using a pastry brush, butter the bottoms and sides of the ramekins, making sure to coat all the corners and ridges. Butter all the way to the rim of the ramekins using upward strokes to help the soufflés rise in the oven.

Next, place 1 tsp of sugar in each of the ramekins. Coat the entire ramekin with the sugar, making sure to cover all the butter by tapping and turning the ramekin. Dump out the excess sugar. Place the ramekins on a baking sheet. There should be at least an inch of space between the ramekins to help with airflow in the oven.

Now let's make the soufflés! First, we need to make a blackberry compote by cooking the blackberries on the stove. Place the blackberries into a medium-sized saucepan along with the vanilla, sugar, and 1 Tbsp of water. Turn the heat to medium, and when the berries start to simmer, cook the mixture for 18 minutes until the berries have released their juices, are soft, and the sauce has thickened some. Stir occasionally.

Transfer the compote to a food processor or a blender, and blend the berries for a few moments to ensure they are smooth. Then press the compote through a sifter to remove the seeds. Pour the compote into a bowl, and place it in the freezer to cool.

Now let's separate the 6 eggs and make the pastry cream, which is the base of our soufflé. Place 4 of the egg yolks in a medium-sized saucepan and the 6 egg whites into a medium-sized mixing bowl. Discard the excess 2 yolks.

Into the 4 egg yolks, add the flour and half-and-half. Mix until combined. Heat the mixture over medium heat, whisking constantly,

Prepared ramekin

Consistency of blackberry compote when ready to take off the stove

until it has thickened and is similar to the thickness of a pudding.

Take the pastry cream off the heat and press it through a fine sifter to remove any bits of cooked egg. Then add the butter, and whisk until incorporated.

Take the blackberry compote out of the freezer, and mix it into the pastry cream.

Now grab your egg whites. Add the cream of tartar, and whip the egg whites on medium speed until they are white and foamy. Then increase your speed to high, and continue whipping until they reach stiff peaks. You will know you have reached stiff peaks when you can pick the beaters up and the peaks of egg whites stand straight.

Fold a third of the egg whites into your blackberry pastry cream mixture until mostly incorporated. Then fold in the remainder of the egg whites.

Once fully combined, divide the soufflé batter between the 8 ramekins. I like to use a very large serving spoon to do this.

Place the baking sheet in the 425°F oven, and IMMEDIATELY decrease the oven temp to 375°F. Bake the soufflés for 16–17 minutes until they are well risen, the edges are set, and the center wobbles ever so slightly. Avoid opening the oven door while the soufflés are baking so that you do not collapse them. The only thing that can collapse a soufflé is a rapid drop in temperature, which is why they deflate soon after they come out of the oven.

As soon as the soufflés come out of the oven, they need to be eaten. They will deflate within a few minutes of being taken out of the oven.

Eat them right out of the ramekins with a spoon.

Enjoy your blackberry soufflés!

Egg whites whipped to stiff peaks

Portioned out soufflé batter

Strawberry Soufflés

Ingredients:

12 oz. strawberries

1 tsp vanilla

4 Tbsp sugar

4 egg yolks

2 Tbsp all-purpose flour

1 c. half-and-half

2 Tbsp butter

6 egg whites

1/8 tsp cream of tartar

Ramekins:

2 Tbsp butter, softened

8 tsp sugar

PREHEAT 425°F

BAKE 375°F

Bake: 16–17 minutes

Yield: 8 individual soufflés

Make sure you enjoy your soufflés moments after they come out of the oven.

Soufflés are eaten in their ramekins.

These strawberry soufflés have a wonderful pink color.

Special Equipment:

8-oz. ramekins (8 count)

Preheat your oven to 425°F.

First, we need to prepare the ramekins. Divide the 2 Tbsp of softened butter between the 8 ramekins. Using a pastry brush, butter the bottoms and sides of the ramekins, making sure to coat all the corners and ridges. Butter all the way to the rim of the ramekins using upward strokes to help the soufflés rise in the oven.

Next, place 1 tsp of sugar in each of the ramekins. Coat the entire ramekin with the sugar, making sure to cover all the butter by tapping and turning the ramekin. Dump out the excess sugar. Place the ramekins on a baking sheet. There should be at least an inch of space between the ramekins to help with airflow in the oven.

Now let's make the soufflés! First, we need to make a strawberry compote by cooking the strawberries on the stove. Cut the tops off the strawberries, halve them, and place them into a medium-sized saucepan along with the vanilla, sugar, and 1 Tbsp of water. Turn the heat to medium, and when the berries start to simmer, cook the mixture for 18 minutes, until the berries have released their juices, are soft, and the sauce has thickened some. Stir occasionally.

Transfer the compote to a food processor or a blender, and blend the berries for a few moments to ensure they are smooth. Then press the compote through a sifter to remove the seeds. Pour the compote into a bowl, and place it in the freezer to cool.

Now let's separate the 6 eggs and make the pastry cream, which is the base of our soufflé. Place 4 of the egg yolks in a medium-sized saucepan and the 6 egg whites into a medium-sized mixing bowl. Discard the excess 2 yolks.

Into the 4 egg yolks, add the flour and half-and-half. Mix until combined. While whisking constantly, heat the mixture over medi-

Prepared ramekin

Consistency of strawberry compote when ready to take off the stove

um heat until it has thickened and is similar to the thickness of a pudding.

Take the pastry cream off the heat and press it through a fine sifter to remove any bits of cooked egg. Then add the butter, and whisk until incorporated.

Consistency of pastry cream when ready to take off the stove

Take the strawberry compote out of the freezer, and mix it into the pastry cream.

Now grab your egg whites. Add the cream of tartar, and whip the egg whites on medium speed until they are white and foamy. Then increase your speed to high, and continue whipping until they reach stiff peaks. You will know you have reached stiff peaks when you can pick the beaters up and the peaks of egg whites stand straight.

Fold a third of the egg whites into your strawberry pastry cream mixture until mostly incorporated. Then fold in the remainder of the egg whites.

Egg whites whipped to soft peaks

Once fully combined, divide the soufflé batter between the 8 ramekins. I like to use a very large serving spoon to do this.

Place the baking sheet in the 425°F oven, and IMMEDIATELY decrease the oven temp to 375°F. Bake the soufflés for 16–17 minutes, until they are well risen, the edges are set, and the center wobbles ever so slightly.

Avoid opening the oven door while the soufflés are baking so that you do not collapse them. The only thing that can collapse a soufflé is a rapid drop in temperature, which is why they deflate soon after they come out of the oven.

Egg whites whipped to stiff peaks

As soon as the soufflés come out of the oven they need to be eaten. They will deflate within a few minutes of being taken out of the oven.

Eat them right out of the ramekins with a spoon.

Enjoy your strawberry soufflés!

Fontina Soufflé

Ingredients:

3 Tbsp butter
3 1/2 Tbsp all-purpose flour
1 c. half-and-half
3 oz. fontina
4 egg yolks
1/2 tsp salt
1/2 tsp pepper
1 tsp mustard
5 egg whites
1/8 tsp cream of tartar

Ramekins:

1 Tbsp butter, softened
Parmesan cheese

PREHEAT 425°F
BAKE 375°F
Bake: 35–36 minutes
Yield: 4-5 servings
This is a lovely savory dinner soufflé.
Make sure you enjoy your soufflé moments after it comes out of the oven. This soufflé is wonderfully creamy.

Special Equipment:
48-oz. ramekins

Preheat your oven to 425°F.

First, we need to prepare our large ramekin. Using a pastry brush, take about 1 Tbsp of softened butter and brush it around the ramekin, making sure to butter all the corners and ridges. Butter all the way to the rim of the dish using upward strokes to help the soufflé rise in the oven. Next, place some Parmesan cheese in the ramekin. Tap the Parmesan all around the ramekin, making sure to coat all the butter with the cheese. Dump out the excess Parmesan.

Now, let's make the soufflé! First, we need to make a simple white sauce on the stove. To do this, place 3 Tbsp butter in a skillet and melt it on medium heat.

Once melted, add the flour. Stirring constantly, cook the flour until it no longer smells like raw flour and looks very bubbly. While whisking, add the half-and-half. Continue whisking until the sauce becomes very thick, much thicker than a typical white sauce. Transfer the white sauce to another bowl, and allow to cool slightly. Meanwhile, grate the cheese and set aside.

Now let's separate the 5 eggs. You will need 5 egg whites but only 4 egg yolks.

Add the yolks to the white sauce along with the salt, pepper, and mustard. Mix to combine.

Now let's whip the egg whites. Add the cream of tartar, and whip the egg whites on medium speed until they are white and foamy. Then increase your speed to high, and continue to whip until you reach stiff peaks. You will know you have reached stiff peaks when you can pick the beaters up and the peaks of egg whites stand straight.

Consistency of white sauce when ready to take off the stove

Egg whites whipped to stiff peaks

Fold a third of the egg whites into the white sauce until mostly incorporated, then fold in the remainder of the egg whites. Once the egg whites are mostly incorporated, add the grated cheese and continue to fold until mixed.

If you would like, you can pause the process here, cover the mixing bowl, and leave the soufflé batter in the fridge to bake later, but the final texture of the soufflé will be saucier in the middle. If you put the soufflé in the fridge, it may add a few extra minutes to the bake time.

Pour your soufflé batter into the prepared ramekin. Place the ramekin into the 425°F oven, and IMMEDIATELY decrease the temperature to 375°F. Bake for 35–36 minutes, until the soufflé is well risen and has a slight wobble to it. Avoid opening the oven door while the soufflé is baking so that you do not collapse it. The only thing that can collapse a soufflé is a rapid drop in temperature, which is why it will deflate soon after it comes out of the oven.

As soon as the soufflé comes out of the oven, it needs to be plated and eaten. It will deflate within a few minutes of being taken out of the oven.

Enjoy your fontina soufflé!

Gruyère Soufflé

Ingredients:

3 Tbsp butter
3 1/2 Tbsp all-purpose flour
1 c. half-and-half
3 oz. Gruyère
4 egg yolks
1/2 plus 1/8 tsp salt
3/4 tsp pepper
1 1/4 tsp mustard
5 egg whites
1/8 tsp cream of tartar

Ramekins:
1 Tbsp butter, softened
Parmesan cheese

PREHEAT 425°F
BAKE 375°F
Bake: 34 minutes
Yield: 4–5 servings
This is a lovely savory dinner soufflé.
Make sure you enjoy your soufflé moments after it comes out of the oven. This soufflé is creamy and flavorful.

Special Equipment:
48-oz. ramekins

Preheat your oven to 425ºF.

First, we need to prepare our large ramekin. Using a pastry brush, take about 1 Tbsp of softened butter and brush it around the ramekin, making sure to butter all the corners and ridges. Butter all the way to the rim of the dish using upward strokes to help the soufflé rise in the oven. Next, place some Parmesan cheese in the ramekin. Tap the Parmesan all around the ramekin, making sure to coat all the butter in the cheese. Dump out the excess Parmesan.

Consistency of white sauce when ready to take off the stove

Now, let's make the soufflé! First, we need to make a simple white sauce on the stove. To do this, place your butter in a skillet, and melt it on medium heat.

Once melted, add the flour. Stirring constantly, cook the flour until it no longer smells like raw flour and looks very bubbly. While whisking, add the half-and-half. Continue whisking until the sauce becomes very thick, much thicker than a typical white sauce. Transfer the white sauce to another bowl, and allow to cool slightly. Meanwhile, grate the cheese and set aside.

Egg whites whipped to stiff peaks

Now let's separate the 5 eggs. You will need 5 egg whites but only 4 egg yolks.

Add the yolks to the white sauce along with the salt, pepper, and mustard. Mix to combine.

Now let's whip the egg whites. Add the cream of tartar, and whip the egg whites on medium speed until they are white and foamy. Then increase your speed to high, and continue to whip until you reach stiff peaks. You will know you have reached stiff peaks when you can pick the beaters up and the peaks of egg whites stand straight.

Fold a third of the egg whites into the white sauce until mostly incorporated, then fold in the remainder of the egg whites. Once the egg whites are mostly incorporated, add the grated cheese and continue to fold until mixed.

If you would like, you can pause the process here, cover the mixing bowl, and leave the soufflé batter in the fridge to bake later, but the final texture of the soufflé will be saucier in the middle. If you put the soufflé in the fridge, it may add a few extra minutes to the bake time.

Pour your soufflé batter into the prepared ramekin. Place the ramekin into the 425°F oven, and IMMEDIATELY decrease the temperature to 375°F. Bake for 34 minutes, until the soufflé is well risen and has a slight wobble to it. Avoid opening the oven door while the soufflé is baking so that you do not collapse it. The only thing that can collapse a soufflé is a rapid drop in temperature, which is why it will deflate soon after it comes out of the oven.

As soon as the soufflé comes out of the oven, it needs to be plated and eaten. It will deflate within a few minutes of being taken out of the oven.

Enjoy your Gruyère soufflé!

Havarti & Gruyère Soufflé

Ingredients:

3 Tbsp butter
3 1/2 Tbsp all-purpose flour
1 c. half-and-half
1.5 oz. creamy Havarti
1.5 oz. Gruyère
4 egg yolks
1/2 plus 1/8 tsp salt
3/4 tsp pepper
1 1/4 tsp mustard
5 egg whites
1/8 tsp cream of tartar

Ramekins:
1 Tbsp butter, softened
Parmesan cheese

PREHEAT 425°F
BAKE 375°F
Bake: 34 minutes
Yield: 4-5 servings
This is a lovely savory dinner soufflé.
Make sure you enjoy your soufflé moments after it comes out of the oven.
This soufflé is flavorful and creamy.

Special Equipment:
48-oz. ramekins

Preheat your oven to 425ºF.

First, we need to prepare our large ramekin. Using a pastry brush, take about 1 Tbsp of softened butter and brush it around the ramekin, making sure to butter all the corners and ridges. Butter all the way to the rim of the dish using upward strokes to help the soufflé rise in the oven. Next, place some Parmesan cheese in the ramekin. Tap the Parmesan all around the ramekin, making sure to coat all the butter with the cheese. Dump out the excess Parmesan.

Now, let's make the soufflé! First, we need to make a simple white sauce on the stove. To do this, place your butter in a skillet and melt it on medium heat.

Once melted, add the flour. Stirring constantly, cook the flour until it no longer smells like raw flour and looks very bubbly. While whisking, add the half-and-half. Continue whisking until the sauce becomes very thick, much thicker than a typical white sauce. Transfer the white sauce to another bowl, and allow to cool slightly. Meanwhile, grate the cheeses and set aside.

Now let's separate the 5 eggs. You will need 5 egg whites but only 4 egg yolks.

Add the yolks to the white sauce along with the salt, pepper, and mustard. Mix to combine.

Now let's whip the egg whites. Add the cream of tartar, and whip the egg whites on medium speed until they are white and foamy. Then increase your speed to high, and continue to whip until you reach stiff peaks. You will know you have reached stiff peaks when you can pick the beaters up and the peaks of egg whites stand straight.

Consistency of white sauce when ready to take off the stove

Egg whites whipped to stiff peaks

Fold a third of the egg whites into the white sauce until mostly incorporated, then fold in the remainder of the egg whites. Once the egg whites are mostly incorporated, add the grated cheeses and continue to fold until mixed.

If you would like, you can pause the process here, cover the mixing bowl, and leave the soufflé batter in the fridge to bake later, but the final texture of the soufflé will be saucier in the middle. If you put the soufflé in the fridge, it may add a few extra minutes to the bake time.

Pour your soufflé batter into the prepared ramekin. Place the ramekin into the 425°F oven, and IMMEDIATELY decrease the temperature to 375°F. Bake for 34 minutes, until the soufflé is well risen and has a slight wobble to it. Avoid opening the oven door while the soufflé is baking so that you do not collapse it. The only thing that can collapse a soufflé is a rapid drop in temperature, which is why it will deflate soon after it comes out of the oven.

As soon as the soufflé comes out of the oven, it needs to be plated and eaten. It will deflate within a few minutes of being taken out of the oven.

Enjoy your Havarti and Gruyère soufflé!

Cheddar Soufflé

Ingredients:

3 Tbsp butter
3 1/2 Tbsp all-purpose flour
1 c. half-and-half
3 oz. sharp cheddar
4 egg yolks
1/2 plus 1/8 tsp salt
3/4 tsp pepper
1 1/4 tsp mustard
5 egg whites
1/8 tsp cream of tartar

Ramekins:

1 Tbsp butter, softened
Parmesan cheese

PREHEAT 425°F
BAKE 375°F
Bake: 31–32 minutes
Yield: 4–5 servings
This is a lovely savory dinner soufflé. Make sure you enjoy your soufflé moments after it comes out of the oven. This soufflé is incredibly delicious and is my favorite dinner soufflé.

Special Equipment:
48-oz. ramekins

Preheat your oven to 425ºF.

First, we need to prepare our large ramekin. Using a pastry brush, take about 1 Tbsp of softened butter and brush it around the ramekin, making sure to butter all the corners and ridges. Butter all the way to the rim of the dish using upward strokes to help the soufflé rise in the oven. Next, place some Parmesan cheese in the ramekin. Tap the Parmesan all around the ramekin, making sure to coat all the butter with the cheese. Dump out the excess Parmesan.

Now, let's make the soufflé! First we need to make a simple white sauce on the stove. To do this, place your butter in a skillet and melt it on medium heat.

Once melted, add the flour. Stirring constantly, cook the flour until it no longer smells like raw flour and looks very bubbly. While whisking, add the half-and-half. Continue whisking until the sauce becomes very thick, much thicker than a typical white sauce. Transfer the white sauce to another bowl, and allow to cool slightly. Meanwhile, grate the cheese and set aside.

Now let's separate the 5 eggs. You will need 5 egg whites but only 4 egg yolks.

Add the yolks to the white sauce along with the salt, pepper, and mustard. Mix to combine.

Now let's whip the egg whites. Add the cream of tartar, and whip the egg whites on medium speed until they are white and foamy. Then increase your speed to high, and continue to whip until you reach stiff peaks. You will know you have reached stiff peaks when you can pick the beaters up and the peaks of egg whites stand straight.

Consistency of white sauce when ready to take off the stove

Egg whites whipped to stiff peaks

Fold a third of the egg whites into the white sauce until mostly incorporated, then fold in the remainder of the egg whites. Once the egg whites are mostly incorporated, add the grated cheese and continue to fold until mixed.

If you would like, you can pause the process here, cover the mixing bowl, and leave the soufflé batter in the fridge to bake later, but the final texture of the soufflé will be saucier in the middle. If you put the soufflé in the fridge, it may add a few extra minutes to the bake time.

Pour your soufflé batter into the prepared ramekin. Place the ramekin into the 425°F oven, and IMMEDIATELY decrease the temperature to 375°F. Bake for 31–32 minutes, until the soufflé is well risen and has a slight wobble to it. Avoid opening the oven door while the soufflé is baking so that you do not collapse it. The only thing that can collapse a soufflé is a rapid drop in temperature, which is why it will deflate soon after it comes out of the oven.

As soon as the soufflé comes out of the oven, it needs to be plated and eaten. It will deflate within a few minutes of being taken out of the oven.

Enjoy your cheddar soufflé!

Pastries

Croissants

Ingredients:

Dough:
4 2/3 c. bread flour
1/2 Tbsp salt
1/4 c. sugar
1 pkg instant yeast (7 grams)
3/4 c. plus 2 Tbsp water
1/2 c. milk
1/4 c. butter, chilled

Butter block:
1 1/2 c. butter (3 sticks), chilled

Egg wash:
1 egg yolk
1 Tbsp heavy cream

BAKE 375°F

Knead: 5 minutes in a stand mixer
Rest #1: 10 minutes
Knead: 8–10 minutes in stand mixer
Rise #1: 45–60 minutes (on counter)
Rise #2: 4 hours (in fridge)
Rest #2: 20 minutes (in freezer)
Chill #1: 45 minutes
Chill #2: 45 minutes
Chill #3: 45 minutes
Chill #4: overnight
Rise #3: 2–2 1/2 hours
Bake: 31 minutes

Yield: 8 croissants

Making croissants is a 2-day project. Allow 9 1/2 hours the first day and 3 1/2 hours the second day.

In a stand mixer, mix together the flour, salt, sugar, and yeast, making sure to add the salt and yeast on separate sides of the bowl. Then add the water and milk. Using a dough attachment knead the mixture for about 5 minutes, until the dough becomes a bit smoother. The dough may look dry at first, but it will hydrate. Next, let the dough rest for 10 minutes to relax the gluten molecules and allow the flour to hydrate.

After the rest, cut the chilled butter into 1/4-Tbsp cubes. Add the cold butter to the dough all at once, and continue to knead until the butter is fully incorporated and the dough is smooth and no longer sticky.

Scrape the dough out of the bowl, and form it into a ball. Slash the dough fairly deep in a plus shape. Slashing the dough like this will cause the dough to rise in a square shape, making it easier to roll out into a rectangle later. Place the dough in a greased bowl, drape a wet towel over the bowl, and leave the dough to rise on the counter until it rises to 1 1/2 times its original size, about 45–60 minutes.

After this first rise on the counter, transfer the bowl to the fridge, and allow to rise for 4 hours.

While the dough is rising in the fridge, and with at least an hour of rising time left, let's make the butter block. First, cut a piece of parchment paper so that you have one large piece of parchment paper that can encase your 3 sticks of butter. Make small marks on the parchment paper outlining the sides and corners of an 8 × 8 square. Next, crease the parchment along those marks. Center your 3 sticks of butter inside the 8 × 8 square. The 3 sticks should be touching. Fold the excess parchment paper over the sticks of butter to encase them, making sure that you still have an 8 × 8 square of parchment.

The dough a bit smoother after kneading for 5 minutes

The smooth non-sticky dough after adding the butter and finishing kneading

Slashed dough ready for its first rise on the counter

Now, with the sticks of butter horizontal to you, bash the butter with a rolling pin to fuse the sticks of butter together. Continue bashing and rolling the butter until it reaches the edges and corners of our 8 × 8 packet of parchment paper. Place the parchment-encased butter in the fridge to chill.

Once the dough is done rising in the fridge, take the dough out, place it on a work surface, and form the dough into a rough square using the corners of the dough we got from slashing it.

Place the dough on a long piece of plastic wrap, and fold the plastic wrap over the dough so that you create an 8 × 8 square of plastic wrap. Fold in the edges of the plastic wrap to create a sealed package. Using a rolling pin, roll the dough so that it fills up the 8 × 8 package of plastic wrap. Place the plastic-wrapped dough in the freezer for 20 minutes.

After 20 minutes, take out both the dough and the butter. Unwrap the dough, and place it on a floured counter. Roll the dough out into a 16 × 8-inch rectangle. Brush off any excess flour.

Now, let's encase the butter in the dough. Remove the butter block from the parchment, and center it on the dough. The width of the butter block might be slightly smaller than the width of the dough.

Take the top length of the dough, and pull it over the butter toward the middle. Then, take the lower length of the dough, and pull it up toward the middle of the butter so the ends of the dough meet but do not overlap.

Now rotate the dough so that the seam is vertical to you. Beat the dough with the rolling pin a little bit to flatten it. Then roll the dough out to 24 inches long. The dough

Creased parchment paper

Completed butter block

8 by 8 square of dough wrapped in plastic wrap ready to chill in the frig

Butter block encased in the dough

should be 1/4 inch thick. While you are rolling the dough out, be sure it is not sticking to the counter by lifting it off the counter and dusting with flour as needed.

For the next several steps, we are going to laminate the dough. We will do what is called a book fold once, then a letter fold twice, chilling the dough in between each of these turns. Doing 1 book fold and 2 letter folds yields a flaky croissant that is softer. If you would like an even flakier croissant, do 2 book folds, then 1 letter fold.

Taking the 24-inch slab of dough, let's do the book fold. Take the top length and pull it down toward the middle. Then take the bottom length and pull it up toward to the middle, leaving a small gap between the 2 edges of dough. Then fold the dough in half, parallel to the small gap. Wrap the dough in plastic wrap and transfer the dough to the fridge for 45 minutes to chill.

Once the dough is finished chilling, it is time to do a letter fold. Take the dough out of its plastic wrap and place it on a floured counter with the short side parallel to you. Beat the dough a little bit to flatten it, then roll the dough out into a slab again that is 24 inches long and 8 inches wide. Make sure the dough is not sticking to the counter by flouring as needed. Now, we are going to fold the dough like a letter. Take the bottom third of the dough and pull it up over the middle third. Then, taking the top third of dough, fold it down and over to fully overlap the middle section. Wrap the dough in plastic wrap again, and leave to chill in the fridge for 45 minutes.

Once chilled, take the dough out of the fridge to do another letter fold. After you do the second letter fold, wrap the dough in plastic wrap again and chill the dough for 45 minutes in the fridge.

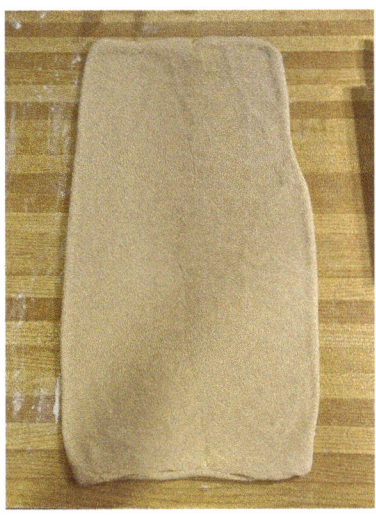

Dough rolled out to 24 inches long and one-quarter inch thick

Book fold part 1 – folding the top and bottom in towards the middle with a small gap

Book fold part 2 – completed book fold

Once it is done chilling, take the dough out of the fridge, unwrap it, and place it on a floured surface. Roll the dough out into a 14 × 17-inch rectangle. Then transfer the dough to a baking sheet. Place plastic wrap over the surface of the dough and return to the fridge to chill overnight. Tomorrow we will roll and bake the croissants!

The next day, simmer some water on the stove in a saucepan. Once the water just barely reaches a simmer, put the pan in a cold oven. This will create a warm and steamy environment for our croissants to rise very well in.

Take the 14 × 17-inch slab of dough, and place it on a floured counter. Make sure the dough is still 14 × 17 inches. If not, roll out the dough a little more to meet those dimensions. Then trim the 14-inch side of the dough so that the sides are straight. The dough should be 14 × 16 inches once you trim the 14-inch side.

Using a pizza cutter, cut the dough into 4 sections that are each 4 inches wide. Next, using a ruler to help guide you along a straight line, cut each of the rectangles into 2 triangles. Trim the flat short side of the triangles so that you have an isosceles triangle by starting at right angle corner and cutting a straight line across.

Line 2 baking sheets with parchment paper. You will put 4 croissants on each baking sheet.

Now it is time to roll the croissants! Starting at the short flat side of the triangle, gently lengthen the corners. Then gently pick up the long triangle to slightly lengthen it. Now roll up the triangle into a croissant shape starting at the short flat side. Once rolled up, place the croissant on the prepared baking sheet, making sure the point of the croissant is slightly tucked underneath the croissant.

Letter fold part 1 – folding the bottom third up to cover the middle third of the dough

Letter fold part 2 – completed letter fold flipped seamside down

Dough rolled out to 14 by 17 inches

It is important to tuck the tip underneath, otherwise the croissant will unroll when it rises and bakes. Repeat this process with the other 7 triangles.

Once all the croissants are rolled, drape plastic wrap over the croissants. Next, check the temperature of the steamed oven. The oven should be barely warm and no more than 70°F. If it is hotter than this, you will melt the butter in the croissants. If the oven is too hot, leave the door open for a couple moments to cool it. Place the baking sheets of croissants in the steamed oven, and leave to rise for 2 to 2 1/2 hours until the croissants have doubled in size and are puffy and very wobbly.

Once the croissants have risen, take them out of the oven and discard the plastic wrap. Then place the baking sheets in the freezer to resolidify the butter before baking. Remove the saucepan of water from the oven and preheat to 375°F.

In the meantime, prepare the egg wash. Use a fork to mix together 1 egg yolk and 1 Tbsp of heavy cream. This creates an excellent egg wash.

Once the oven has preheated, take the croissants out of the freezer. Brush each of the croissants with the egg wash using a pastry brush. Make sure you only brush the top flat surfaces of the croissants. Do not brush egg wash on the sides as this will fuse the layers together, restricting the layers from expanding in the oven.

Place the baking sheets in the oven, and bake the croissants for 31 minutes or until the croissants are dark golden brown in color.

Enjoy your croissants!

Slab of dough trimmed and cut into 8 triangles

Trimming the flat short side of the triangle to become an isosceles triangle

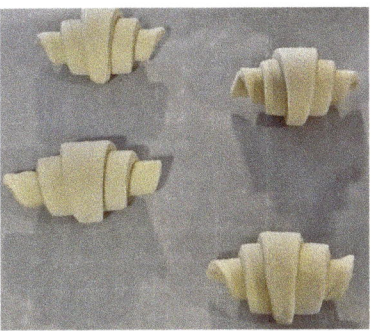

Rolled up croissants before their final rise

Croissants doubled in size after their final rise

Macarons

Ingredients:

80g almond flour
80g powdered sugar
40g granulated sugar
50g egg whites
Dash of cream of tartar
Gel or powdered food
coloring (optional)

Special Equipment:
Scale
2 silicone baking mats

BAKE 280°F

Rest: 30–45 minutes

Bake: 16–18 minutes

Yield: 16 macarons

If you want to color your macarons, you must use gel or powdered food coloring.

High humidity will affect your macarons due to their moisture sensitivity, resulting in a flat macaron.

If filling your macarons with a soft filling, pipe a firmer filling as a border around the outer edge.

Use silicone baking mats to help lift off your macarons after baking.

First, sift the almond flour and the powdered sugar together into a small mixing bowl. Then measure out the granulated sugar into a separate bowl so that it is ready to use. If you would like to flavor the macarons chocolate, take a small amount of the mixture out with a spoon and replace it with cocoa powder

Amount of almond flour powerdered sugar mixture to remove and replace with cocoa powder to flavor the macarons chocolate

Next, place the egg whites into a small or medium-sized bowl, and add the cream of tartar. Whip the egg whites on medium speed until they reach soft peaks. You will know you have reached soft peaks when you can pick up the beaters and the peaks of egg whites bend over.

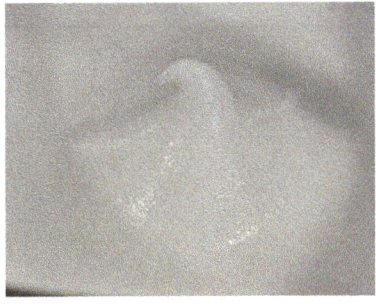

Egg whites whipped to soft peaks

Once you reach this stage, with the mixer running add the sugar in a steady stream or in 3 portions, mixing between each addition. Once all the sugar has been incorporated, continue whipping the egg whites on high speed until they reach stiff peaks. You will know that you have reached stiff peaks when you can pick up the beaters and the peaks of egg whites stand straight.

Egg whites whipped to stiff peaks (with food coloring)

Pour a third of the almond flour mixture over the egg whites, and fold together until mostly incorporated. Then add the remainder of the mixture, and fold until combined.

Now we are going to macaronage. This is the most important step in the process of making macarons. To macaronage, we will begin with the motion of folding. Using a spatula, scrape around the bowl, gathering the batter, starting at one o'clock and ending at twelve o'clock; then, taking the flat part of the spatula, smear the batter around the bowl. Our goal is to deflate the egg whites. Without this step being done properly, your macarons will be hollow on the inside.

Repeat the scrape-and-smear motion several times until you reach the consistency we

Macaronaging part 1 – scraping around the bowl

are looking for, testing the batter frequently. To test the batter, use the spatula to pick up the batter and let it fall off the spatula. If the stream of batter breaks off easily, you need to keep macaronaging; the batter is too thick. The consistency we want is for the batter to pour off the spatula relatively slowly but without breaking off. You do not want the batter to run off the spatula, though, because that means you have overmacaronaged, and your macarons will be flat.

During the macaronaging, before the mixture has reached the proper consistency, you can add gel food coloring if desired. It is important to use either gel coloring or powdered coloring. Macarons are extremely sensitive to moisture, and using liquid food coloring will result in flat macarons.

Now we are ready to pipe the macarons! Line 2 baking sheets with silicone baking mats or parchment paper. We will pipe 16 cookies per sheet.

Transfer the macaron batter to a piping bag or plastic zipper bag, and snip off the tip so that the hole is about 1/4 inch wide. Holding the piping bag at an angle, pipe small 1-inch circles, making sure the cookies are 1–2 inches apart.

Once you have piped all 32 cookies, it is time to bang the pans. This will both spread the cookies and burst any air bubbles within the cookies. Rap the sheets on the counter until the cookies have spread to about 1 1/2 in wide and any obvious air bubbles have burst. Once you are done rapping the pan on the counter, if there are any other bubbles near the surface of the cookies, burst them with a toothpick.

Preheat the oven to 280°F.

Macaronaging part 2 – smearing around the bowl

Proper consistency of batter after macaronaging

We need to leave the macarons to dry out a little bit and form a film on top. If you do not do this step, the macarons will erupt like little volcanos in the oven. Rest the macarons for 30–45 minutes. You will know they are done resting when you can brush your finger over the top of the cookies and it does not leave an imprint or stick to your finger.

Now we are ready to bake the macarons! Bake them for 16–18 minutes. There are a couple tests you can do to tell if they are done baking. The first is to use a metal spatula turned upside down to gently squish the feet of the macaron. The "feet" refers to the ruffly bottom portion of the macaron. If it squishes, they need a minute longer. If it does not squish, they are done baking. Another way to test for doneness is to gently wiggle the top of the macaron. If the top wiggles on its feet, the macarons are not done and need one more minute. If the macaron is firm when you wiggle, they are done.

As soon are the macarons are done baking, take them out of the oven and immediately slide the silicone baking mat or parchment paper off the baking sheet and onto the counter. Let the macarons cool like this.

Once the macarons are fully cool, gently lift them off the silicone mat or parchment paper. If they are not releasing, use a spatula to get them off. If the macarons pop right off, that means they were baked perfectly.

To fill the macarons, pipe your desired filling on the bottom of one of the cookies, then sandwich with another cookie. Fill with anything you'd like such as jams or buttercream frostings or fruit curds.

Enjoy your macarons!

Piped macarons before banging the pan

Piped macarons after banging the pan

Vanilla Cream Puffs

Ingredients:

1 c. plus 5 1/2 tsp all-purpose flour
1/2 c. water
1/2 c. milk
8 Tbsp butter
2 tsp sugar
1 vanilla bean (optional)
4 eggs
1 Tbsp vanilla

Special Equipment:
Instant-read
thermometer

BAKE 400°F
DROP TEMP TO 350°F
Bake: 15 minutes at 400°F
Bake: 17 minutes 350°F
Yield: 16 cream puffs
These cream puffs look gorgeous
when you add the vanilla bean.
Enjoy the wonderful vanilla aroma!

Measure the flour into a separate bowl so that it is ready to use.

Place the water, milk, butter, and sugar into a saucepan. If you would like to use a vanilla bean, add it here as well. To use a vanilla bean, cut it into 2 halves along the length. Using the knife, in one motion slide the knife down each bean half, scraping out the tiny vanilla beans. Add these tiny beans to the saucepan.

Over medium heat, stirring occasionally with a spatula or wooden spoon, heat the mixture until it is simmering. Then add the flour, and mix vigorously until the choux pastry comes together, so it no longer sticks to the sides of the pan, and it forms a ball when you stir. Take the choux pastry off the heat, and allow to cool to below 140°F.

Preheat the oven to 400°F while the choux pastry is cooling.

Once the mixture has cooled down a bit, it is time to add the eggs. You can mix them in by hand or use a mixer. Add the eggs one at a time, mixing each one into the choux pastry almost completely before adding the next. Once the eggs are incorporated, add the vanilla and mix to combine.

Line 2 baking sheets with parchment paper.

Now it is time to pipe the choux pastry. Fill a piping bag or a gallon plastic zipper bag with the pastry. Snip the tip of the piping bag off to create a hole that is about 1/2-inch wide.

Pipe the choux pastry in small mounds that are about 1 1/2 to 2 inches across. Pipe each cream puff 2 inches apart. They will puff up in the oven.

Place the baking sheets in the 400°F oven, and bake them for 15 minutes. Then decrease the

Vanilla choux pastry when done cooking on the stove

Piped vanilla cream puffs

temperature to 350°F, and bake the cream puffs for another 17 minutes. You do not want to open the oven door while the cream puffs are baking, or you will collapse them. The cream puffs should be a golden brown when they are done baking.

Take them out of the oven, and let them cool fully on a wire rack. When you're ready to fill your cream puffs, cut the tops off, make sure the inside is hollow, fill with your desired filling, and replace the tops!

Fill with any filling you'd like, from ice cream to crème pat to whipped cream!

Enjoy your vanilla cream puffs!

Vanilla cream puffs when done baking

Chocolate Cream Puffs

Ingredients:

Vanilla choux pastry:
1/2 c. plus 1 1/2 tsp all-purpose flour
1/4 c. water
1/4 c. milk
4 Tbsp butter
1 tsp sugar
2 eggs
1 tsp vanilla

Chocolate choux pastry:
1/2 c. plus 1 tsp all-purpose flour
3 Tbsp cocoa powder
1/4 c. plus 1 Tbsp water

BAKE 400°F
DROP TEMP TO 350°F
Bake: 15 minutes at 400°F
Bake: 17–19 minutes at 350°F
Yield: 16 cream puffs
These cream puffs have a beautiful swirl.
These chocolate cream puffs pair nicely with a chocolate mascarpone.

1/4 c. milk
4 Tbsp butter
4 tsp sugar
2 eggs
1 tsp vanilla

Special Equipment:
Instant-read thermometer

For this recipe, we will make 2 types of choux pastry: chocolate and vanilla.

First, let's prepare the vanilla!

Measure out the flour in a separate bowl so that it is ready to use.

Into a saucepan, place the water, milk, butter, and sugar. Over medium heat, stirring occasionally with a spatula or wooden spoon, heat the mixture until it is simmering. Then add the flour, and mix vigorously until the choux pastry comes together, so it no longer sticks to the sides of the pan, and it forms a ball when you stir. Take the vanilla choux pastry off the heat, and allow to cool to below 140°F.

Preheat the oven to 400°F while the choux pastry is cooling.

While the vanilla choux pastry is cooling, let's get started on the chocolate choux pastry.

Into a small bowl, whisk together the flour and cocoa powder and set aside.

Into a saucepan, place the water, milk, butter, and sugar. Over medium heat, stirring occasionally with a spatula or wooden spoon, heat the mixture until it is simmering. Then add the flour mixture, and mix vigorously until the choux pastry comes together, so it no longer sticks to the sides of the pan, and it forms a ball when you stir. Take the chocolate choux pastry off the heat, and allow to cool to below 140°F.

Once the vanilla choux pastry is cool, it is time to add the 2 eggs. You can mix them in by hand or use a mixer. Add the eggs one at a time, mixing each one into the choux pastry almost completely before adding the next. Once the eggs are incorporated, add the vanilla

Vanilla choux pastry when done cooking on the stove

Chocolate choux pastry when done cooking on the stove

and mix to combine. Scrape the vanilla choux pastry into a piping bag or a quart plastic zipper bag. Snip the tip of the bag off so that you have a hole a quarter of an inch wide.

By now, the chocolate choux pastry should be cool, and we can add the eggs. Add the eggs one at a time, mixing each one almost completely into the choux pastry before adding the next. Once the eggs are incorporated, add the vanilla and mix to combine. Transfer the chocolate choux pastry into a piping bag or a quart plastic zipper bag. Snip the tip of the bag off so that you have a hole a quarter of an inch wide.

Place both the vanilla and chocolate piping bags into another bigger piping bag or into a gallon plastic zipper bag. The vanilla and chocolate piping bags should be evenly placed inside the larger bag so that one is not lower than the other. Snip off the tip of the large piping bag off so that the hole is half an inch wide. Now you are ready to pipe the cream puffs!

Line 2 baking sheets with parchment paper.

As you pipe the choux pastry, apply more pressure to the chocolate side of the piping bag, as this choux pastry is a bit thicker. Pipe the choux pastry in small mounds that are about 1 1/2 to 2 inches across. Pipe each cream puff 2 inches apart. They will puff up in the oven. Each mound will have a swirl of chocolate and vanilla!

Place the baking sheets in the 400°F oven and bake them for 15 minutes. Then decrease the temperature to 350°F and bake the cream puffs for another 17–19 minutes. You do not want to open the oven door while the cream puffs are baking, or you will collapse them. The creams puffs should be a golden brown when they are done baking.

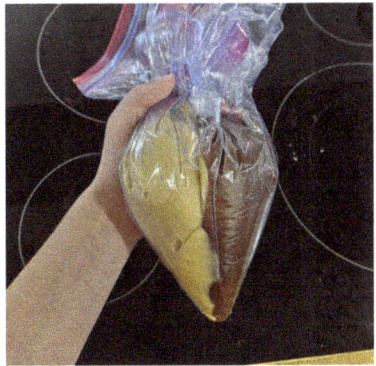

Vanilla and chocolate choux pastry piping bags together in another piping bag

Piped chocolate cream puffs

Take them out of the oven, and let your cream puffs cool fully on a wire rack. When you're ready to fill your cream puffs, cut the tops off, make sure the inside is hollow, fill with your desired filling, and replace the tops.

Fill with any filling you'd like, from ice cream to pudding to chocolate mascarpone.

Enjoy your chocolate cream puffs!

Cinnamon Cream Puffs

Ingredients:

1 1/2 tsp cinnamon
1 1/4 c. plus 2 Tbsp all-purpose flour
1/2 c. water
1/2 c. milk
8 Tbsp butter
2 Tbsp sugar
4 eggs
2 tsp vanilla

Special Equipment:
Instant-read
thermometer

BAKE 400°F
DROP TEMP TO 350°F
Bake: 15 minutes at 400°F
Bake: 18–19 minutes at 350°F
Yield: 16 cream puffs
These cinnamon cream puffs pair nicely with an apple filling.
These cream puffs have a wonderful speckled appearance.

In a small bowl, whisk together the cinnamon and the flour and set aside.

Measure out into a saucepan the water, milk, butter, and sugar. Over medium heat, stirring occasionally with a spatula or wooden spoon, heat the mixture until it is simmering. Then add the flour, and mix vigorously until the choux pastry comes together, so it no longer sticks to the sides of the pan, and it forms a ball when you stir. Take the choux pastry off the heat, and allow to cool to below 140°F.

Preheat the oven to 400°F while the choux pastry is cooling.

Once the mixture has cooled down a bit, it is time to add the eggs. You can mix them in by hand or use a mixer. Add the eggs one at a time, mixing each one almost completely into the choux pastry before adding the next. Once the eggs are incorporated, add the vanilla and mix to combine.

Line 2 baking sheets with parchment paper.

Now it is time to pipe the choux pastry. Fill a piping bag or a gallon plastic zipper bag with the choux pastry. Snip the tip of the piping bag off to create a hole that is about 1/2-inch wide.

Pipe the choux pastry in small mounds that are about 1 1/2 to 2 inches across. Pipe each cream puff 2 inches apart. They will puff up in the oven.

Place the baking sheets in the 400°F oven, and bake them for 15 minutes. Then decrease the temperature to 350°F, and bake the cream puffs for another 18–19 minutes. You do not want to open the oven door while the cream puffs are baking, or you will collapse them. The cream puffs should be a golden brown when they are done.

Cinnamon choux pastry when done cooking on the stove

Piped cinnamon cream puffs

Cinnamon cream puffs when done baking

Take them out of the oven, and let your cream puffs cool fully on a wire rack. When you're ready to fill your cream puffs, cut the tops off, make sure the inside is hollow, fill with your desired filling, and replace the tops.

Fill with any filling you'd like, from ice cream to pudding to an apple crème pat.

Enjoy your cinnamon cream puffs!

Orange Cream Puffs

Ingredients:

1 1/4 c. all-purpose flour
1/2 c. water
1/2 c. milk
8 Tbsp butter
2 Tbsp sugar
1/2 tsp salt
4 eggs
4 tsp orange emulsion

Special Equipment:
Instant-read
thermometer

BAKE 400°F
DROP TEMP TO 350°F
Bake: 15 minutes at 400°F
Bake: 17–19 minutes at 350°F
Yield: 16 cream puffs
You will need orange emulsion for this recipe. You cannot substitute with orange juice or extract. These orange cream puffs pair nicely with a cranberry whipped cream.

Measure out the flour so that it is ready to use, and set aside.

Into a saucepan, place the water, milk, butter, sugar, and salt. Over medium heat, stirring occasionally with a spatula or wooden spoon, heat the mixture until it is simmering. Then add the flour, and mix vigorously until the choux pastry comes together, so it no longer sticks to the sides of the pan, and it forms a ball when you stir. Take the choux pastry off the heat, and allow to cool to below 140°F.

Preheat the oven to 400°F while the choux pastry is cooling.

Once the mixture has cooled down a bit, it is time to add the eggs. You can mix them in by hand or use a mixer. Add the eggs one at a time, mixing each one almost completely into the choux pastry before adding the next. Once the eggs are incorporated, add the orange emulsion and mix to combine.

Line 2 baking sheets with parchment paper.

Now it is time to pipe the choux pastry. Fill a piping bag or a gallon plastic zipper bag with the choux pastry. Snip the tip of the piping bag off to create a hole that is about 1/2-inch wide.

Pipe the choux pastry in small mounds that are about 1 1/2 to 2 inches across. Pipe each cream puff 2 inches apart. They will puff up in the oven.

Place the baking sheets in the 400°F, oven and bake them for 15 minutes. Then decrease the temperature to 350°F, and bake the cream puffs for another 17–19 minutes. You do not want to open the oven door while the cream puffs are baking, or you will collapse them. The creams puffs should be a golden brown when they are done baking.

Choux pastry when done cooking on the stove

Piped orange cream puffs

Orange cream puffs when done baking

Take them out of the oven, and let your cream puffs cool fully on a wire rack. When you're ready to fill your cream puffs cut the tops off, make sure the inside is hollow, fill with your desired filling, and replace the tops.

Fill with any filling you'd like, from ice cream to pudding to cranberry whipped cream.

Enjoy your orange cream puffs!

Éclairs

Ingredients:

Choux pastry:
1 1/4 c. all-purpose flour
2 tsp sugar
1/2 c. water
1/2 c. milk
8 Tbsp butter
1 vanilla bean (optional)
4 eggs
1 Tbsp vanilla

Chocolate glaze:
4 oz. semisweet baking chocolate (56% cacao)
1/2 c. whipping cream

BAKE 400°F
DROP TEMP TO 350°F
Bake: 10 minutes at 400°F
Bake: 16 minutes at 350°F
Yield: 35 éclairs
Fill your éclairs with a light crème légère.
Optionally, use a 1/2-inch star piping tip to create a nice pattern on the exterior of your éclairs.

Special Equipment:
Instant-read thermometer

Measure out the flour so that it is ready to use, and set aside.

Place into a saucepan the sugar, water, milk, and butter. If you would like to use a vanilla bean, add it here as well. To use a vanilla bean, cut it into 2 halves along the length. Using the knife, in one motion slide the knife down each bean half, scraping out the tiny vanilla beans. Add these tiny beans to the saucepan.

Over medium heat, stirring occasionally with a spatula or wooden spoon, heat the mixture until it is simmering. Then add the flour, and mix vigorously until the choux pastry comes together, so it no longer sticks to the sides of the pan, and it forms a ball when you stir. Take the choux pastry off the heat, and allow to cool to below 140°F.

Preheat the oven to 400°F while the choux pastry is cooling.

Once the mixture has cooled down a bit, it is time to add the eggs. You can mix them in by hand or use a mixer. Add the eggs one at a time, mixing each one almost completely into the choux pastry before adding the next. Once the eggs are incorporated, add the vanilla and mix to combine.

Line 2 baking sheets with parchment paper.

Now it is time to pipe the choux pastry. Fill a piping bag or a gallon plastic zipper bag with the choux pastry. Snip the tip of the piping bag off to create a hole that is about 1/2-inch wide.

In one motion, pipe the choux pastry in stripes that are 3/4-inch wide and 3 to 3 1/2 inches long. Pipe each éclair 1 1/2 inches apart.

Choux pastry when done cooking on the stove

Piped éclairs

Place the baking sheets in the 400°F oven, and bake them for 10 minutes. Then decrease the temperature to 350°F, and bake the éclairs for another 16 minutes. You do not want to open the oven door while the éclairs are baking, or you will collapse them. The éclairs should be a golden brown when they are done baking. Let your éclairs cool fully.

My favorite filling to fill eclairs with is a crème légère, but you can fill them with any light filling you'd like such as whipped cream.

When you're ready to fill your éclairs, you can fill them one of two ways. One way is to cut them in half horizontally, fill them, and replace the top half. Another option is to poke 2 holes in the top of the éclair—1 toward the right side of the éclair and 1 toward the left side of the éclair—then fill the éclair through these 2 holes. When you coat the éclair in chocolate, these holes will be covered up. If you would like to dip your éclairs in chocolate, I recommend the second way.

Now it is time to make a chocolate glaze and coat the éclairs! To make the glaze, break the chocolate into small chunks, and place in a bowl. Next, warm the cream in the microwave or on the stove. The cream should be hot but not boiling. Pour the hot cream over the chocolate, and let sit for 2 minutes to melt the chocolate. Then whisk the chocolate and cream together until it makes a smooth ganache. The chocolate glaze is now ready.

After you have filled your éclairs, dip the tops one at a time in the chocolate glaze so that the filling holes are covered up. If needed, use a knife to remove excess chocolate. The éclairs are ready!

Eat your éclairs right away, or wait till the chocolate sets.

Enjoy your éclairs!

Éclairs when done baking

The 2 holes to fill the éclairs on the left and right ends

Prepared chocolate glaze

Craquelin Choux

Ingredients:

Choux pastry:
1 c. plus 5 1/2 tsp all-purpose flour
1/2 c. water
1/2 c. milk
8 Tbsp butter
2 tsp sugar
4 eggs

Craquelin topping:
4 oz. light brown sugar
4 oz. butter, chilled
4 oz. all-purpose flour

BAKE 375°F
Bake: 28–30 minutes
Yield: 18 choux buns
Craquelin choux pastry pairs nicely with a crème pat or a caramel crème pat.
Craquelin choux buns are best eaten the day they are made.

Special Equipment:
Instant-read thermometer

First, let's make the choux pastry. Measure out the flour so that it is ready to use, and set aside.

Measure out into a saucepan the water, milk, butter, and sugar. Over medium heat, stirring occasionally with a spatula or wooden spoon, heat the mixture until it is simmering. Then add the flour, and mix vigorously until the choux pastry comes together, so it no longer sticks to the sides of the pan, and it forms a ball when you stir. Take the choux pastry off the heat, and allow to cool to below 140°F.

Preheat the oven to 375°F while the choux pastry is cooling.

Once the mixture has cooled down a bit, it is time to add the eggs. You can mix them in by hand or use a mixer. Add the eggs one at a time, mixing each one almost completely into the choux pastry before adding the next.

Transfer the choux pastry to a piping bag or a gallon plastic zipper bag with the choux pastry. Snip the tip of the piping bag off to create a hole that is about 1/2-inch wide.

Now let's make the craquelin topping. Place the light brown sugar into a small or medium-sized mixing bowl. Cut the cold butter into cubes, and add to the brown sugar.

Beat by hand or with a mixer until you have a thick, smooth paste. Then add the flour, and continue to mix until a crumbly dough forms. Taking the dough in your hands, form it into a ball.

Place a medium-sized piece of parchment paper on your counter, and set your ball of dough on it. Using your hands, press the dough out into a rough 6 × 8-inch rectangle. Place a second piece of parchment paper on top of the dough, and use a rolling pin to roll the dough out so that it is 1/8 inch thick.

Choux pastry when done cooking on the stove

Choux pastry after adding all the eggs

Butter and light brown sugar beaten together into a smooth paste

Now we need to chill the dough slightly. Place the parchment-covered dough onto a baking sheet, and put in the freezer for 5 minutes.

While the dough is chilling, line another baking sheet with parchment paper.

Once the dough is cold, remove it from the freezer and place on the counter. Now we are going to cut out 2-inch circles to place on top of our choux pastry when we pipe it. Take off the top piece of parchment paper, and use a 2-inch cookie cutter to cut out 18 circles.

Using a small metal spatula, transfer each of the circles to the other lined baking sheet, and place in the freezer while you pipe the choux pastry.

Line 2 baking sheets with parchment paper.

Pipe the choux pastry in small mounds that are about 1 1/2 to 2 inches across. Pipe each choux bun 2 inches apart. They will puff up in the oven.

Once you are done piping the choux puns, remove the craquelin topping from the freezer. Place one little round craquelin topping on each choux bun.

Transfer the choux buns to the oven, and bake for 28–30 minutes, until the craquelin choux is a dark golden brown. Fully cool the craquelin choux on a wire rack before filling.

When you're ready to fill your craquelin choux, poke a hole in the bottom of each bun. Using a piping bag fitted with a piping tip, fill the bun with your filling.

Fill with a caramel crème pat or another filling of your choice.

Enjoy your craquelin choux!

The craquelin topping between 2 pieces of parchment paper rolled out to one-eighth inch thickness

Piped choux pastry

Craquelin topping placed on top of piped choux pastry

Pâte Sucrée

Ingredients:

8 Tbsp butter, softened
1/4 c. sugar
1/8 tsp salt
1 1/3 c. all-purpose flour
1 egg yolk
1 tsp vanilla
1 Tbsp heavy cream

Yield: 1 9-inch pie crust or 8 tartlet shells

Pâte sucrée makes an excellent pie crust for any sweet pie or cheesecake.

Double this recipe if you are making a pie with a lattice crust or a lid.

In the bowl of a stand mixer, cream the softened butter for 30 seconds. Add the sugar and salt, and beat until creamed. Add the flour and beat until combined. The mixture will be pretty crumbly. Add the egg yolk, vanilla, and the heavy cream. Mix until a dough forms.

Turn the dough out onto a very lightly floured counter, and gently press the dough together to incorporate any dry crumbs. Form the dough into a ball. Wrap the dough in plastic wrap, and let rest in the fridge for 30 minutes before using.

The dough is now ready to be used in any way you'd like, such as to make lemon tartlets or as the base for your next cheesecake!

On a floured counter roll out the dough to the dimensions needed for your recipe, making sure to periodically lift the dough and re-flour as needed to prevent sticking.

To fully bake this recipe as a 9-inch pie crust shell, preheat the oven to 325°F. Place the rolled-out dough into your pie dish. The dough may break, but simply press it back together to repair it. Trim the crust half an inch beyond the edge of the pie dish. Prick the surface, and place the pie dish onto a baking sheet for easy mobility. Bake in the oven for 20 minutes. The crust will be a light golden brown.

As soon as the crust is out of the oven, trim the overhanging dough to create a smooth edge.

To partially blind bake this recipe for a 9-inch crust, preheat the oven to 325°F. Follow the instructions above for how to place the dough in the pie dish. Then bake the crust for 16 minutes.

Crumbly dough after adding the flour

Finished pâte sucrée dough ready to roll out

Pâte sucrée in a 9-inch pie dish

To partially blind bake this recipe for a 4-inch tartlet, preheat the oven to 325°F. Place the dough in the tart tins as per your recipe. Then prick the bottom surface, and bake the crust for 12–14 minutes, until it is beginning to look dry but is still very pale in color. After this partial bake, fill with your desired filling and follow the temperature and bake time that your recipe recommends. If the crust is getting too dark, place some foil over the edges.

Enjoy your pâte sucrée!

Lemon Tartlets

Ingredients:

Pâte sucrée:
8 Tbsp butter, softened
1/4 c. sugar
1/8 tsp salt
1 1/3 c. all-purpose flour
1 egg yolk
1 tsp vanilla
1 Tbsp heavy cream

Lemon filling:
3/4 c. lemon juice, 4–10 lemons
1 Tbsp lemon zest
3/4 c. sugar
8 Tbsp butter
4 whole eggs
4 egg yolks

Meringue topping:
4 egg whites
1/8 tsp cream of tartar
1/8 tsp salt
1/2 c. sugar
1/2 tsp vanilla

BLIND BAKE 325°F
BAKE 350°F
Bake tart crusts: 12–14 minutes at 325°F
Bake filled tarts: 8–9 minutes at 350°F

Yield: 8 tartlets
The sweetened meringue pairs nicely with the tart lemon. Make sure you save your extra egg whites from the lemon filling to use for the meringue.

Special Equipment:
4-inch tart rings (8 count)

The first step in this recipe is to make the pâte sucrée crust.

Preheat the oven to 325°F.

In the bowl of a stand mixer, cream the softened butter for 30 seconds. Add the sugar and salt, and beat until creamed. Add the flour and beat until combined. The mixture will be pretty crumbly. Add the egg yolk, vanilla, and heavy cream. Mix until a dough forms.

Turn the dough out onto a floured counter, and gently press the dough together to incorporate any dry crumbs. Form the dough into a ball. Wrap the dough in plastic, and place in the freezer for a few minutes while you zest and juice the lemons.

Take 2 of your lemons, and finely grate them until you have 1 Tbsp of zest. Then juice them so that you get 3/4 cup juice. Add both the zest and the juice to a saucepan.

Take your dough from the freezer, and flour your counter. Roll the dough out into a rough rectangle to a thickness of 1/8 inch, making sure to periodically lift the dough and reflour as needed to prevent sticking. Using the 4-inch tart rings, cut out 8 circles. You will have a lot of excess dough. Place the circles on a piece of parchment paper, and set aside.

Place your 8 tart rings on a baking sheet in an organized way.

Gather the excess dough and roll it into a rectangle that is 8–9 inches wide and 10–11 inches long. Trim the dough so that you have straight sides, but make you sure you end up with a rectangle that is at least 8 × 10 inches in size.

Crumbly dough after adding the flour

Finished pâte sucrée dough ready to roll out

The 8 cut out circles disks

Cut 8 strips of dough that are each 1 inch wide and 10 inches long. Carefully take one strip of dough at a time, making sure to support the middle while lifting it, and place the strip of dough inside one of the tart rings. Gently position the strip of dough so that it lines the inside wall of the tart ring. If the strip of dough rips while you are lining the tart ring, you can simply repair it by using your fingers to fuse the break back together.

Once the strip of dough is inside the tart ring against the inner wall, you should have some overlap where the ends meet. To trim the excess, gently take a butter knife and cut the excess dough off, leaving a very small amount of overlap. Using your fingers, fuse this seam together to seal the dough.

Once you have placed all 8 strips of dough into the tart rings, it is time to add the bottom disks.

Working one disk at a time, place each disk inside a tart ring. The disk will be slightly larger than the ring. Press the edges of the disk to fuse with the dough wall to seal the dough. Make sure you are pressing the dough into an even layer so that the corners of the tart rings are not too thick.

Once all 8 disks have been added to the tart rings, you are ready to prick the bottoms of the tartlets. Prick the bottoms, then place the baking sheet in the freezer for a few minutes.

Before we blind bake the tartlets, let's get the filling going. Into the saucepan that has the lemon juice and zest, add the sugar, butter, 4 whole eggs, and 4 egg yolks. Set the 4 egg whites aside in a medium-sized bowl to use later for the meringue. Set the lemon mixture aside to begin baking the tartlets.

Take the baking sheet of tartlets out of the

Trimmed dough cut into 8 1-inch strips

Tartlet rings lined with the strips of dough

Fully lined tartlet rings

freezer, and place them in the 325°F oven to blind bake for 12–14 minutes, until they are beginning to look dry but are still very pale in color.

While the tartlets are baking, turn your attention back to the lemon filling. Turn the heat to medium, and while whisking constantly from the moment you turn the heat on, cook the mixture until it gets thick, bubbly, and passes the spoon test. A spoon test indicates that the mixture is ready when the mixture coats the back of a spoon and you can make a stripe with your finger that does not re-flood in.

By the time the lemon filling is ready, the tartlets should be almost done blind baking. Once they are done, take the baking sheet out of the oven and place it on the counter or stovetop. Increase the oven temperature to 350°F.

Take the lemon filling, and spoon into each of the tartlets evenly. The tarts will not be full to the brim. Once the oven is up to temp, place the baking sheet back in the oven and bake for another 8–9 minutes to set the curd. To tell whether or not the tartlets are done, gently jiggle a tartlet. It should be set at the edges but have a slight wobble in the middle. You want to be careful when baking the tartlets to not boil the curd. They should not be in the oven longer than 9 minutes.

Take the tartlets out of the oven, and place the baking sheet on a cooling rack while you make the meringue topping. Remove the tart rings from around the tartlets. They should just lift right off. Turn off the oven.

Place the egg whites in a bowl and add the cream of tartar and salt. Whip the egg whites on medium speed until they reach soft peaks. You will know you have reached soft peaks

Blind baked tartlet shells

Successful spoon test

Lemon tartlets when done baking

when you can pick up the beaters and the peaks of egg whites bend over.

Once you reach this stage, with the mixer running, add the sugar in a steady stream or in 3 portions, mixing in between each addition. Once all the sugar is incorporated, add the vanilla and continue whipping until the meringue reaches stiff peaks. You will know you have reached stiff peaks when you can pick the beaters up and the peaks of egg whites stand straight.

Transfer the meringue to a piping bag or a plastic zipper bag fitted with a piping tip, and you are ready to pipe the meringue onto the lemon tartlets. This will be more meringue than you need, so feel free to do whatever meringue design you like!

Once you have piped meringue onto all 8 of your tartlets, it is time to torch the meringue. If you have a cooking blowtorch, you can use it to brown the meringue. If you don't have one, use the broiler in the oven to brown the meringue. To do this, set the oven to broil, and place the baking sheet of tarts into the oven. It is fine if the oven is not cool when you do this. Watch the meringue closely as it will brown quickly. The final color of the meringue should be a splotchy golden brown. Once you are happy with the color of the meringue, take the tartlets out of the oven and they are ready.

Enjoy your lemon tartlets!

Meringue egg whites whipped to soft peaks

Meringue egg whites whipped to stiff peaks

Apple Tartlets

Ingredients:

Pâte sucrée:
8 Tbsp butter, softened
1/4 c. sugar
1/8 tsp salt
1 1/3 c. all-purpose flour
1 egg yolk
1 tsp vanilla
1 Tbsp heavy cream

Apple filling:
2 Granny Smith apples
1 Tbsp butter
1/2 tsp cinnamon
1/4 tsp nutmeg
1 1/3 c. water
6 Tbsp all-purpose flour

BLIND BAKE 325°F
BAKE 350°F
Bake tart crusts: 12–14 minutes at 325°F
Bake filled tarts: 8 minutes at 350°F
Yield: 8 tartlets
The creamy smooth crème pâtissière pairs nicely with the apple filling.

1/8 tsp salt
1/4 c. sugar

Topping:
Crème pâtissière

Special Equipment:
4-inch tart rings (8 count)

The first step in this recipe is to make the pâte sucrée crust.

Preheat the oven to 325°F.

Into the bowl of a stand mixer, place the softened butter and cream for 30 seconds. Add the sugar and salt, and beat until creamed. Add the flour and beat until combined. The mixture will be pretty crumbly. Add the egg yolk, vanilla, and the heavy cream. Mix until a dough forms.

Crumbly dough after adding the flour

Turn the dough out onto a floured counter, and gently press the dough together to incorporate any dry crumbs. Form the dough into a ball. Wrap in plastic, and place in the fridge for a few minutes while you prepare the apples.

First, peel both apples. I've found that using a potato peeler makes the process quick and easy. Then core the apples. If your apple corer also slices the apples, that's great; otherwise, slice each apple into 8 pieces. Taking 1 slice at a time, position it like a boat, and cut it lengthwise either in half or in thirds, depending on the width of the apple slice. Holding the pieces together in the boat shape, turn it onto its side and cut the apple slices along their length either in half or in thirds. Then finish by dicing the slices perpendicular to the previous cut. Add the diced apples to a medium-sized saucepan.

Finished pâte sucrée dough ready to roll out

Take your dough from the freezer, and flour your counter. Roll the dough out into a rough rectangle to a thickness of 1/8 inch, making sure to periodically lift the dough and reflour as needed to prevent sticking. Using the 4-inch tart rings, cut out 8 circles. You will have a lot of excess dough. Place the circles on a piece of parchment paper, and set aside.

Diced apples

Place your 8 tart rings on a baking sheet in an organized way.

Gather the excess dough, and roll it into a rectangle that is 8–9 inches wide and 10–11 inches long. Trim the dough so that you have straight sides but make you sure you end up with a rectangle that is at least 8 × 10 inches in size.

Cut 8 strips of dough that are each 1 inch wide and 10 inches long. Carefully take one strip of dough at a time, making sure to support the middle while lifting it, and place the strip of dough inside one of the tart rings. Gently position the strip of dough so that it lines the inside wall of the tart ring. If the strip of dough rips while you are lining the tart ring, you can simply repair it by using your fingers to fuse the break back together.

Once the strip of dough is inside the tart ring against the inner wall, you should have some overlap where the ends meet. To trim the excess, gently take a butter knife and cut the excess dough off, leaving a very small amount of overlap. Using your fingers, fuse this seam together to seal the dough.

Once you have placed all 8 strips of dough into the tart rings, it is time to add the bottom disks.

Working one disk at a time, place each disk inside a tart ring. The disk will be slightly larger than the ring. Press the edges of the disk to fuse with the dough wall to seal the dough. Make sure you are pressing the dough into an even layer so that the corners of the tart rings are not too thick.

Once all 8 disks have been added to the tart rings, you are ready to prick the bottoms of the tartlets. Prick the bottoms, then place the baking sheet in the freezer for a few minutes.

The 8 cut out circles disks

Trimmed dough cut into 8 1-inch strips

Tartlet rings lined with the strips of dough

Before we blind bake the tartlets, let's get the filling going. Into the pot that has the diced apples in it, add the butter, cinnamon, nutmeg, water, flour, salt, and sugar. Give a brief stir, and set aside for a moment.

Take the baking sheet of tartlets out of the freezer, and place them in the 325°F oven to blind bake for 12–14 minutes, until they are beginning to look dry but are still very pale in color.

Fully lined tartlet rings

While the tartlets are baking, turn your attention back to the apple filling. Over medium heat, stirring often, cook the mixture until it thickens and passes the spoon test. A spoon test indicates that the mixture is ready when the mixture coats the back of a spoon and you can make a stripe with your finger that does not re-flood in.

By now, the tartlet shells should be almost done blind baking. Once they are done, take the baking sheet out of the oven and place it on the counter or stovetop. Increase the oven temperature to 350°F.

Fill each of the tartlets evenly with the apple filling. Once the oven is up to temp, place the baking sheet back in the oven and bake for another 8 minutes to set the apple filling.

Blind baked tartlet shells

Take the tartlets out of the oven, transfer to a cooling rack, and cool fully before adding the topping.

Make the topping as the tarts are cooling. For the topping we will make a crème pâtissière.

2 c. milk
1/3 c. sugar
3 Tbsp cornstarch
1/8 tsp salt
4 egg yolks
2 Tbsp butter
1 tsp vanilla

Successful spoon test

Into a medium-sized saucepan place the milk, sugar, cornstarch, salt, and egg yolks. Over medium heat, while stirring constantly, heat the mixture until it becomes thick and starts bubbling big bubbles. Once there are big bubbles, cook the mixture for 1 more minute to ensure that the crème pat will thicken as it cools, then remove from the heat.

Place a fine strainer or sieve over a bowl, and strain the crème pat through it to remove any bits of cooked egg.

Add the butter and mix until combined, then add in the vanilla. Let cool on the counter or in the fridge, or speed up the process by using an ice bath.

Here's how to prepare an ice bath. Grab a bowl that is larger than your bowl of crème pat. Fill the bowl with water then with ice cubes, leaving room to put your crème pat bowl into the bowl of ice and water. Place your crème pat bowl into the ice bath, and whisk the crème pat to cool it down. It will cool down quickly.

Once cool, transfer the crème pat to a piping bag fitted with the piping tip of your choice. Pipe whatever design you would like on your apple tartlets.

Enjoy your apple tartlets!

Fully baked tartlets

Lime Tartlets

Ingredients:

Pâte sucrée:
8 Tbsp butter, softened
1/4 c. sugar
1/8 tsp salt
1 1/3 c. all-purpose flour
1 egg yolk
1 tsp vanilla
1 Tbsp heavy cream

Lime filling:
3/4 c. lime juice, 8–12 limes
1 Tbsp lime zest
3/4 c. sugar
8 Tbsp butter
4 whole eggs
4 egg yolks

Cream topping:
250g whipping cream

BLIND BAKE 325°F
BAKE 350°F
Bake tart crusts: 12–14 minutes at 325°F
Bake filled tarts: 8–9 minutes at 350°F
Yield: 8 tartlets
The light whipped cream pairs beautifully with the tart lime.
The creaminess of a whipped cream topping complements the flavor of lime better than a meringue topping.

54g powdered sugar
1 tsp vanilla

Special Equipment:
4-inch tart rings (8 count)

The first step in this recipe is to make the pâte sucrée crust.

Preheat the oven to 325°F.

Into the bowl of a stand mixer, place the softened butter and cream for 30 seconds. Add the sugar and salt, and beat until creamed. Add the flour and beat until combined. The mixture will be pretty crumbly. Add the egg yolk, vanilla, and the heavy cream. Mix until a dough forms.

Turn the dough out onto a floured counter, and gently press the dough together to incorporate any dry crumbs. Form the dough into a ball. Wrap in plastic, and place in the freezer for a few minutes while you zest and juice the limes.

Take your limes, and finely grate them until you have 1 Tbsp of zest. Then juice them so you get 3/4 cup juice. Add both the zest and juice to a saucepan.

Take your dough from the freezer, and flour your counter. Roll the dough out into a rough rectangle to a thickness of 1/8 inch, making sure to periodically lift the dough and reflour as needed to prevent sticking. Using the 4-inch tart rings, cut out 8 circles. You will have a lot of excess dough. Place the circles on a piece of parchment paper, and set aside.

Place your 8 tart rings on a baking sheet in an organized way.

Gather the excess dough, and roll it into a rectangle that is 8–9 inches wide and 10–11 inches long. Trim the dough so that you have straight sides, but make you sure you end up with a rectangle that is at least 8 × 10 inches in size.

Cut 8 strips of dough that are each 1 inch wide and 10 inches long. Carefully take one strip of dough at a time, making sure to sup-

Crumbly dough after adding the flour

Finished pâte sucrée dough ready to roll out

The 8 cut out circles disks

port the middle while lifting it, and place it inside one of the tart rings. Gently position the strip of dough so that it lines the inside wall of the tart ring. If the strip of dough rips while you are lining the tart ring, you can simply repair it by using your fingers to fuse the break back together.

Once the strip of dough is inside the tart ring against the inner wall, you should have some overlap where the ends meet. To trim the excess, gently take a butter knife and cut the excess dough off, leaving a very small amount of overlap. Using your fingers, fuse this seam together to seal the dough.

Once you have placed all 8 strips of dough into the tart rings, it is time to add the bottom disks.

Working one disk at a time, place each disk inside a tart ring. The disk will be slightly larger than the ring. Press the edges of the disk to fuse with the dough wall to seal the dough. Make sure you are pressing the dough into an even layer so that the corners of the tart rings are not too thick.

Once all 8 disks have been added to the tart rings, you are ready to prick the bottoms of the tartlets. Prick the bottoms, then place the baking sheet in the freezer for a few minutes.

Before we blind bake the tartlets, let's get the filling going. Into the saucepan that has the lime juice and zest, add the sugar, butter, 4 whole eggs, and 4 egg yolks.

Take the baking sheet of tartlets out of the freezer, and place them in the 325°F oven to blind bake for 12–14 minutes, until they are beginning to look dry but are still very pale in color.

While the tartlets are baking, turn your attention back to the lime filling. Turn the heat to

Trimmed dough cut into 8 1-inch strips

Tartlet rings lined with the strips of dough

Fully lined tartlet rings

medium, and while whisking constantly from the moment you turn the heat on, cook the mixture until it gets thick, bubbly, and passes the spoon test. A spoon test indicates that the mixture is ready when the mixture coats the back of a spoon and you can make a stripe with your finger that does not re-flood in.

By the time the lime filling is ready, the tartlets should be almost done blind baking. Once they are done, take the baking sheet out of the oven and place it on the counter or stovetop. Increase the oven temperature to 350°F.

Fill each of the tartlets evenly with the lime filling. Once the oven is up to temp, place the baking sheet back in the oven and bake for another 8–9 minutes to set the curd. To tell whether or not the tartlets are done, gently jiggle a tartlet. It should be set at the edges but have a slight wobble in the middle. You want to be careful while baking the tartlets to not boil the curd. They should not be in the oven longer than 9 minutes.

Take the tartlets out of the oven, and transfer to a cooling rack. Remove the tart rings from around the tartlets. They should just lift right off. Cool fully before making the cream topping.

Once the tartlets are fully cool, we can make the cream topping. Into a small or medium-sized mixing bowl, add the whipping cream, powdered sugar, and vanilla. Beat with a hand mixer until it reaches the consistency of whipped cream. Dollop or pipe it onto your tartlets.

Enjoy your lime tartlets!

Blind baked tartlet shells

Successful spoon test

Lime tartlets when done baking

Crème Pâtissière

Ingredients:

2 c. milk
1/3 c. sugar
3 Tbsp cornstarch
1/8 tsp salt
4 egg yolks
2 Tbsp butter
1 tsp vanilla

Yield: 2 cups
Crème pâtissière, also called crème pat or pastry cream, is excellent in any dessert.
A crème pat is smooth and creamy.
A crème pat is incredibly versatile.

Into a medium-sized saucepan place the milk, sugar, cornstarch, salt, and egg yolks. Over medium heat, while stirring constantly, heat the mixture until it becomes thick and starts bubbling big bubbles. Once there are big bubbles, cook the mixture for 1 more minute to ensure that the crème pat will thicken as it cools, then remove it from the heat.

Place a fine strainer or sieve over a bowl, and strain the crème pat through it to remove any bits of cooked egg.

Add the butter and mix until combined. Then add in the vanilla. Let cool on the counter or in the fridge, or speed up the process by using an ice bath.

Here's how to prepare an ice bath. Grab a bowl that is larger than your bowl of crème pat. Fill the bowl with water then with ice cubes, leaving room to put your crème pat bowl into the bowl of ice and water. Place your crème pat bowl into the ice bath, and whisk the crème pat to cool it down. It will cool down quickly.

The crème pat is now ready!

Use it as a filling for a cake or cream puffs or as a topping.

Enjoy your crème pâtissière!

Crème pat bubbling big bubbles

Crème Légère

Ingredients:

2 c. milk
1/3 c. sugar
3 Tbsp cornstarch
1/8 tsp salt
4 egg yolks
2 Tbsp butter
1 tsp vanilla
1 c. whipping cream

Yield: 3 1/2 cups
This crème légère is one of the best fillings for éclairs.
Enjoy this incredibly light and airy filling.
Crème légère is made from a crème pâtissière.

To make a crème légère, we first need to make a crème pat.

Into a medium-sized saucepan, place the milk, sugar, cornstarch, salt, and egg yolks. Over medium heat, while stirring constantly, heat the mixture until it becomes thick and starts bubbling big bubbles. Once there are big bubbles, cook the mixture for 1 more minute to ensure that the crème pat will thicken as it cools.

Take the crème pat off the stove. Place a fine strainer or sieve over a bowl, and strain the crème pat through it to remove any bits of cooked egg.

Add the butter and mix until combined. Add in the vanilla. Let cool on the counter or in the fridge, or speed up the process by using an ice bath.

Here's how to prepare an ice bath. Grab a bowl that is larger than your bowl of crème pat. Fill the bowl with water then with ice cubes, leaving room to put your crème pat bowl into the bowl of ice and water. Place your crème pat bowl into the ice bath, and whisk the crème pat to cool it down. It will cool down quickly.

Next, take the whipping cream and whip it until it is the consistency of whipped cream and is spreadable. Fold in a third of the whipped cream until it is mostly incorporated. Then fold in the remainder of the whipped cream.

Your crème légère is now ready to use for anything you'd like.

Enjoy your crème légère!

Crème pat bubbling big bubbless

Finished crème légère

Lemon Curd

Ingredients:

1 Tbsp lemon zest
3/4 c. lemon juice, 4–10 lemons
3/4 c. sugar
8 Tbsp butter
4 whole eggs
4 egg yolks

Yield: 2 cups
Lemon curd is a great filling for cakes and other desserts. Lemon curd is especially yummy on a pavlova.

First, we need to prepare the lemons. Finely grate your lemons until you have 1 Tbsp of zest. Then juice them so that you get 3/4 cup juice. Add both the zest and the juice to a saucepan.

Into that same pot, add the sugar, butter, 4 whole eggs, and 4 egg yolks. Turn the heat to medium, making sure to whisk constantly from the moment you turn on the heat to prevent the mixture from curdling. Cook the mixture until it gets thick and passes the spoon test. A spoon test indicates that the mixture is ready when the mixture coats the back of a spoon and you can make a stripe with your finger that does not re-flood in. Transfer to another dish to cool.

Your lemon curd is ready for whatever you would like to use it for.

Enjoy your lemon curd!

Successful spoon test

Meringue Topping

Ingredients:

4 egg whites
1/8 tsp cream of tartar
1/8 tsp salt
1/2 c. sugar
1/2 tsp vanilla

Yield: 2 cups
Use meringue as a topping
for lemon meringue pie or for
another dessert.
You can brown meringue with a
cooking blowtorch or with the
broiler function in your oven.

Place the egg whites in a medium-sized bowl, and add the cream of tartar and salt. Whip the egg whites on medium speed until they reach soft peaks. You will know you have reached soft peaks when you pick up the beaters and the peaks of egg whites bend over.

Once you reach this stage, with the mixer running, add the sugar in a steady stream or in 3 portions, mixing between each addition. Once all the sugar is incorporated, add the vanilla and continue whipping until the meringue reaches stiff peaks. You will know you have reached stiff peaks when you pick the beaters up and the peaks of egg whites stand straight.

The meringue is now ready! Use as a topping for a lemon meringue pie or for any other dessert with meringue.

Enjoy your meringue topping!

Egg whites whipped to soft peaks

Egg whites whipped to stiff peaks

Caramel Sauce

Ingredients:

6 Tbsp butter
3/4 c. whipping cream
1 c. sugar
1/4 c. water
1/4 tsp salt
1 tsp vanilla

Yield: 1 3/4 cups
My caramel sauce uses the wet method, resulting in a wonderful depth of flavor. This caramel sauce is easy to make.
The sauce will thicken as it cools but will remain spreadable and useable after being refrigerated.

First, take your butter from the fridge and cut it into 6 pieces so that it is ready to use. Set aside for now. Have your whipping cream easily accessible as well.

Into a medium-sized saucepan with a lid, place the sugar, water, and salt. Stir together to dissolve the sugar. Then brush the sides of the pan with a wet basting brush to rinse them making sure that no sugar remains on the sides of the pan.

When making a wet caramel it is important to prevent crystallization. To do this, we will simply place the lid on the pot. Crystallization is caused by granules of sugar getting on the sides of the pan and cooling. When they fall back into the hot sugar, they crystallize the entire mixture almost instantly. If this happens, the caramel is ruined. It is crucial to dissolve these granules off the sides of the pan. The steam created by having the lid on the pot will do this for you.

The other way you can prevent crystallization is by periodically brushing the sides of the pan with water, but this method is more difficult.

Place the lid on the pot, and turn the heat to high. After a little bit, the caramel will start to brown and begin to look like caramel. As soon as the mixture starts to take on a caramel color, turn the heat to low and remove the lid. The caramel will start to brown very quickly from here.

Continue to cook the mixture until it is a deep amber color. The darker the color of the caramel, the darker the flavor it will have. But you must turn the heat off when tiny, foamy bubbles start to form toward the center of the caramel. If you go beyond this point, you will burn the caramel.

Color of the caramel when it is time to turn down the heat to low

The amber color of the caramel when it is time to add the butter

Once the caramel is at your desired darkness, add the butter all at once. The mixture will bubble rapidly, but this is fine. Whisk vigorously until the butter is all incorporated.

Once the butter is fully incorporated, slowly pour in the cream while whisking constantly. If you need an extra hand to stabilize the pan in order to whisk the caramel, take the pan off the burner and set it on a potholder. This will secure it while you whisk. Continue whisking until the caramel is smooth. Add the vanilla and mix until combined.

Transfer the caramel to another dish, and it is ready to use! The caramel will thicken as it cools. A fun feature of this recipe is that the caramel is still spreadable even when it is chilled.

Enjoy your caramel sauce!

The caramel when you first add the butter

Completed caramel sauce

Caramel Crème Pâtissière

Ingredients:

4 egg yolks
3 Tbsp cornstarch
1/8 tsp salt
2 c. milk
1 c. sugar
1/4 c. water
2 Tbsp butter
1 tsp vanilla

Yield: 2 1/2 cups
Caramel crème pat is a wonderful filling for craquelin choux or any cream puff.
For this recipe we will temper the eggs by adding the hot liquid to the egg yolks while whisking constantly. This is a critical step.
This caramel crème pat has a pleasant light caramel color.

First, place the egg yolks, cornstarch, and salt into a medium-sized, heavy-bottomed bowl. Whisk them together until combined and smooth. Set aside.

Then, place the milk in a small or medium-sized saucepan and warm over medium heat, stirring occasionally to prevent burning. Don't let the milk go beyond a simmer. We do not want to boil the milk, or it will split.

Next we need to make a simple caramel. Into a medium-sized saucepan with a lid, place the sugar and water. Stir together to dissolve the sugar. Then brush the sides of the pan with a wet basting brush to rinse them, making sure that no sugar remains on the sides of the pan.

When making a wet caramel, it is important to prevent crystallization. To do this, we will simply place the lid on the pot. Crystallization is caused by granules of sugar getting on the sides of the pan and cooling. When they fall back into the hot sugar, they crystallize the entire mixture almost instantly. If this happens, the caramel is ruined. It is crucial to dissolve these granules off the sides of the pan. The steam created by having the lid on the pot will do this for you.

The other way you can prevent crystallization is by periodically brushing the sides of the pan with water, but this method is more difficult.

Place the lid on the pot, and turn the heat to high. After a little bit, the caramel will start to brown and begin to look like caramel. As soon as the mixture starts to take on a caramel color, turn the heat to low and remove the lid. The caramel will start to brown very quickly from here.

Continue to cook the mixture until it is a deep amber color. The darker the color of the

Color of the caramel when it is time to turn down the heat to low

The amber color of the caramel when it is done

caramel, the darker the flavor it will have. But you must turn the heat off when tiny, foamy bubbles start to form toward the center of the caramel. If you go beyond this point, you will burn the caramel.

Once the caramel is at your desired darkness, slowly pour the warmed milk into the caramel while whisking constantly. The mixture will bubble rapidly. Whisk until all the caramel is incorporated, and return to a boil over medium heat.

Once the caramel milk is at a boil, pour it into the egg mixture in a small steady stream while whisking the egg mixture constantly. Once all the milk is incorporated, pour the entire mixture back into the saucepan. While whisking constantly, cook the caramel crème pat over medium heat until the mixture is thick and begins to bubble big bubbles. Then cook it for 1 more minute to ensure the mixture will thicken as it cools.

Take the caramel crème pat off the stove. Place a fine strainer or sieve over a bowl, and strain the crème pat through it to remove any bits of cooked egg.

Add the butter and mix until combined. Then add in the vanilla. Let cool on the counter or in the fridge, or speed up the process by using an ice bath.

Here's how to prepare an ice bath. Grab a bowl that is larger than your bowl of crème pat. Fill the bowl with water then with ice cubes, leaving room to put your crème pat bowl into the bowl of ice and water. Place your crème pat bowl into the ice bath, and whisk the crème pat to cool it down. It will cool down quickly. Your caramel crème pat is now ready!

Enjoy your caramel crème pâtissière!

Mixture bubbling big bubbles

*Consistency of caramel crème pat
after cooking 1 more minute*

Cranberry Whipped Cream

Ingredients:

6.5 oz. cranberries
2 c. whipping cream
1/2 c. plus 1 Tbsp
powdered sugar
1 tsp vanilla

Special Equipment:
Scale

Yield: 3 cups
This cranberry whipped cream
is an excellent filling for orange
cream puffs.
The cranberry flavor comes
through beautifully in this
recipe.

Place your cranberries into a small or medium-sized saucepan along with 1 Tbsp of water. Cook the berries over medium heat, stirring often. The cranberries will begin to pop and crackle as they release their juices. Once the mixture has gotten thick and the cranberries are soft, transfer the mixture to a food processor or a blender. Blend until the mixture is smooth.

Consistency of the cranberries when done cooking on the stove

Let the puree cool to room temperature on the counter, or place it in the fridge to cool more quickly.

Once the cranberry puree is cool, measure out a 1/2 cup and place it into a bowl with the whipping cream, powdered sugar, and vanilla. Whip until the mixture is the consistency of whipped cream. Your cranberry whipped cream is now ready!

Enjoy your cranberry whipped cream!

Chocolate Frosting

Ingredients:

8 Tbsp butter, softened
4 c. powdered sugar
3/4 Tbsp cocoa powder
3 Tbsp milk
2 Tbsp hot water
1 tsp vanilla

Yield: 2 cups
This chocolate frosting is fluffy, creamy, smooth, and chocolaty. The hot water "blooms" the cocoa powder creating a deep chocolaty flavor.
The vanilla in this recipe enhances the chocolate flavor.

Place the softened butter into a large bowl. Using a mixer on medium speed, cream the butter for about 20 seconds.

Add the powdered sugar and the cocoa powder, and beat to combine with the butter. Once combined, the mixture will pretty much still look like powdered sugar.

Add the milk, hot water, and vanilla, and continue to beat until the frosting comes together.

The frosting is now ready to use however you'd like.

Enjoy your chocolate frosting!

Chocolate Crémeux

Ingredients:

150g semisweet baking
chocolate (56% cacao)
150g whipping cream
150g milk
3 eggs
90g sugar
1 tsp vanilla

Special Equipment:
Scale

Yield: 2 cups
Chocolate crémeux is a chilled chocolate spread that can be used as a filling or eaten alone.
Chocolate crémeux is rich, silky, and smooth.
Chocolate crémeux needs to be chilled 4–6 hours in the fridge before using.
This chocolate crémeux recipe is sweet, but if you prefer a sweeter crémeux increase the sugar to 120g.

Place the chocolate in a medium-sized bowl.

Into a medium-sized saucepan, place the whipping cream, milk, eggs, and sugar. Over medium heat, while whisking constantly, heat the mixture until it thickens and passes the spoon test. A spoon test indicates that the mixture is ready when the mixture coats the back of a spoon and you can make a stripe with your finger that does not re-flood in.

Take the crémeux off the stove, and pour it over the chocolate. Let sit for a couple of minutes to melt the chocolate. Whisk the mixture until it is smooth, then whisk in the vanilla.

Transfer the crémeux to a shallow dish, and let it set up in the fridge for 4–6 hours until it is fully set, not the least bit runny, and scoopable.

Enjoy your chocolate crémeux!

Successful spoon test

Finished chocolate crémeux ready to chill in the frig

Other Desserts

Macaroons

Ingredients:

14 oz. sweetened
coconut flakes
4 oz. sweetened
condensed milk
1 tsp vanilla
2 egg whites
1/4 tsp salt

Special Equipment:
Food processor

BAKE 325°F

Bake: 20 minutes

Yield: 20 cookies

These cookies are flavorful,
sweet, and light.

These macaroons are great at
a party.

The most important part
of this recipe is blitzing the
coconut properly.

Preheat the oven to 325°F.

First, we need to blitz the coconut. Place the coconut into a food processor. Pulse it in short bursts until the coconut is small and fine but not powdery or mushy.

Blitzed coconut that is small and fine

Place the blitzed coconut into a large mixing bowl, and add the sweetened condensed milk. Mix the coconut and sweetened condensed milk until fully combined. Then add the vanilla, and mix until fully combined.

Next, in a small or medium-sized bowl, whip the egg whites with the salt on medium speed until they are white and foamy. Continue whipping on high speed until you reach stiff peaks. You will know you have reached stiff peaks when you can pick up the beaters and the peaks of egg whites stand straight.

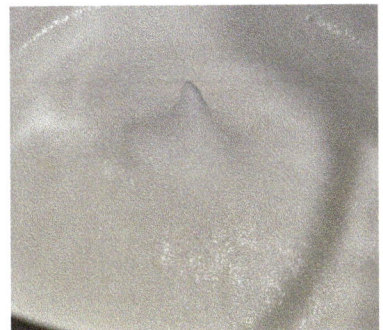

Egg whites whipped to stiff peaks

Fold the egg whites into the coconut mixture until fully combined.

Line 2 baking sheets with parchment paper.

Scoop 1-Tbsp mounds of the batter onto the baking sheet, placing them 1–1 1/2 inches apart. Bake for 20 minutes, until they are golden brown. Cool on a wire rack.

Finished macaroon cookie dough

Enjoy your macaroons!

Macaroon cookies when done baking

Macaroon cookies shaped and ready to bake

Biscotti

Ingredients:

6 Tbsp butter
1/2 c. plus 2 Tbsp sugar
2 eggs
2 tsp vanilla
4 tsp whipping cream
2 1/4 c. all-purpose flour
1/4 tsp salt
2 tsp baking powder
1 1/4 c. almonds,
coarsely chopped

BAKE 325°F
Bake #1: 28 minutes
Bake #2: 15 minutes
Yield: 24 cookies
These biscotti are wonderfully crisp without being dry. They will melt in your mouth.
Enjoy your biscotti at any time of day, even as a breakfast or with tea.

Preheat the oven to 325°F.

In the bowl of a stand mixer or in a bowl with a hand mixer, cream the butter for 30 seconds. Then add the sugar, and beat until fluffy. Add the eggs, vanilla, and whipping cream, and beat until combined.

In a separate bowl, mix together the flour, salt, and baking powder.

Add the flour to the butter mixture, and mix until combined. Add the coarsely chopped almonds, and mix until combined.

Line a baking sheet with parchment paper.

On the lined baking sheet, form the dough into 2 rectangular logs that are roughly 3 inches wide and 3/4 inch thick. Bake the logs for 28 minutes, until golden brown.

Place the logs on a cutting board, and take the parchment off the baking sheet. Let the logs cool for 10 minutes, but no longer. Cooling them beyond 10 minutes will result in overly crumbly logs that are difficult to cut.

Now we will cut the logs into biscotti cookies. Cutting on the diagonal, cut pieces of biscotti that are half an inch thick. The biscotti may be slightly crumbly, but this is okay. Carefully transfer the slices of biscotti onto the baking sheet. You will need 2 baking sheets for all of the biscotti. Bake for another 15 minutes, flipping them halfway through. Transfer the biscotti to a cooling rack.

If you are making multiple batches of biscotti, you must wash and dry your pan after each bake of sliced biscotti so there is no trace of butter on the pan.

Enjoy your biscotti!

Butter and sugar beaten until fluffy

The dough after adding the coarsely chopped almonds

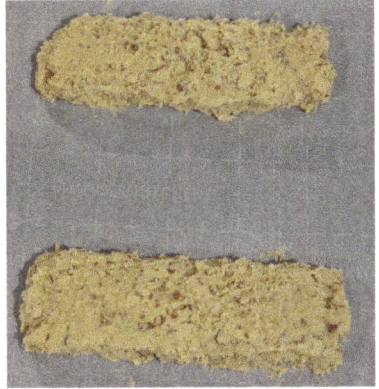

The 2 rectangular logs ready to bake

Pictures continued overleaf

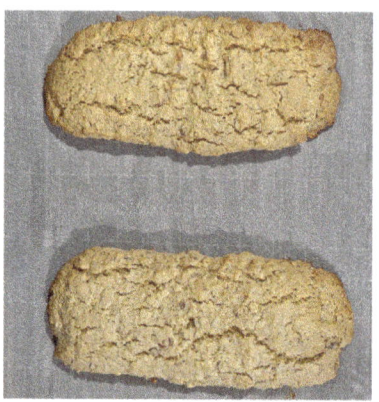

The 2 rectangular logs after baking for 28 minutes

Finished biscotti cookies after their 2nd bake

Flan

Ingredients:

Caramel:
1 c. sugar
2 Tbsp water
Custard:
3 whole eggs
3 egg yolks
1 1/2 c. milk
1 1/2 c. whipping cream
2/3 c. sugar
1 tsp vanilla
1/8 tsp salt

BAKE 325°F
Bake: 70–80 minutes in a 9-inch dish or 28–40 minutes in 8-oz. ramekins.
Yield: 1 9-inch flan or 8 individual flans
Flan is a baked custard and has a smooth texture. This flan is creamy and flavorful.

Special Equipment (optional):
8-oz. ramekins (8 count)

Preheat the oven to 325°F.

If you are making one large flan, set out a 9-inch round cake pan or another flan dish. If you would like to make 8 individual flans, set out 8-oz. ramekins.

Now let's make the caramel! Into a medium-sized saucepan with a lid, place the sugar and water. Stir together to dissolve the sugar. Then brush the sides of the pan with a wet basting brush to rinse them, making sure that no sugar remains on the sides of the pan.

When making a wet caramel, it is important to prevent crystallization. To do this, we will simply place the lid on the pot. Crystallization is caused by granules of sugar getting on the sides of the pan and cooling. When they fall back into the hot sugar, they crystallize the entire mixture almost instantly. If this happens, the caramel is ruined. It is crucial to dissolve these granules off the sides of the pan. The steam created by having the lid on the pot will do this for you.

The other way you can prevent crystallization is by periodically brushing the sides of the pan with water, but this method is more difficult.

Place the lid on the pot, and turn the heat to high. After a little bit, the caramel will start to brown and begin to look like caramel. As soon as the mixture starts to take on a caramel color, turn the heat to low and remove the lid. The caramel will start to brown very quickly from here.

Continue to cook the mixture until it is a deep amber color. The darker the color of the caramel, the darker the flavor it will have. But you must turn the heat off when tiny, foamy bubbles start to form toward the center of the caramel. If you go beyond this point, you

Color of the caramel when it is time to turn down the heat to low

Amber color of the caramel when done

will burn the caramel. Take the caramel off the stove.

To fill a 9-inch dish, pour all the caramel into the dish. Working quickly, tilt the dish so that the caramel coats the entire interior. To fill the little ramekins, pour an eighth of the caramel into one of the ramekins. Working quickly, tilt the ramekin so that the caramel coats the entire interior. Repeat with the other 7 ramekins.

Place your dish or ramekins on a baking sheet that has sides or in a broiler pan. Make sure there is at least 1 inch of space between the ramekins. The flans will not bake properly if they are too close together.

Let's make the custard now. Into a medium-sized bowl, place the whole eggs, egg yolks, milk, whipping cream, sugar, vanilla, and salt. Whisk together until fully combined and smooth, taking care to not whip in much air.

Pour the custard through a sifter or strainer, then pour it into your 9-inch cake pan or divide evenly between your ramekins.

Prepare a kettle of hot water.

Place your baking sheet or broiler pan containing the dish or ramekins onto the oven rack, and pour the hot water into the pan. Fill it as much as the pan will allow but not more than halfway up the ramekins.

Bake for 70–80 minutes if you are making a 9-inch flan or 28–40 minutes for 8-oz. ramekins, until the custard is set. When it is done baking, it should have a slight wobble in the center when you shake the dish.

Caramel poured into ramekins

Important note: There is a bit of a range for the baking time of the little ramekins. I have had the custards fully bake after only 28 minutes and be fully set, but in another oven, the custards have needed a full 40 minutes. After lots of testing, 40 minutes became the time that produced the perfect texture. Don't go beyond 40 minutes when baking the flan. While baking, test it at the 28-minute mark. If it is quite liquid, it will probably need 40 minutes.

Once the flan is done baking, take it out of the oven and let cool until you can place it in the fridge.

Let a 9-inch flan set up in the fridge for 2–4 hours. Let the 8-oz. ramekins set up for at least 2 hours.

To serve the flan, run a knife around the edge of the dish. Place your serving plate on top of the dish and flip the whole thing upside down. Wiggle the dish until the flan releases. Lift off the dish, and the flan is ready!

Enjoy your flan!

Pavlova

Ingredients:

8 egg whites
1 3/4 c. sugar
2 tsp cornstarch
1 tsp cream of tartar
2 tsp vanilla

PREHEAT 300°F
BAKE 225°F
Bake: 80–90 minutes for 1 large pavlova or 75 minutes for 4 mini pavlovas
Yield: 1 large pavlova or 4 mini pavlovas
Pavlova is incredibly easy to make but will require your oven for many hours.
Pavlova is light, fluffy, and delicious.
Top with anything you'd like. My favorite is to top it with whipped cream and lemon curd.

Preheat the oven to 300°F.

Pavlova is very easy to make. Place the egg whites into the bowl of a stand mixer fitted with a whisk attachment. Whip on medium speed until they are white and foamy. Increase the speed to high, and continue to whip until the egg whites reach soft peaks. You will know you have reached soft peaks when you can lift up the whisk and the peaks of egg whites bend over.

Pour in a slow, steady stream of sugar while the mixer is running. Once all the sugar is incorporated, continue whipping on high speed until the egg whites reach stiff peaks and the sugar is fully dissolved. You will know you have reached stiff peaks when you can lift up the whisk and the peaks of egg whites stand straight. For the meringue to be ready, you need to both reach stiff peaks and dissolve all the sugar. Then the egg whites are ready.

Sprinkle the cornstarch, cream of tartar, and vanilla over the egg whites, and fold in until thoroughly combined.

Line a baking sheet with parchment paper. Now we are ready to spread the pavlova onto our lined baking sheet.

You can make one large pavlova or several mini ones. Spread the pavlova onto the parchment paper in an 8-inch disk with a level top. You can frill the edges if desired, using upward strokes with a spatula around the circumference. Or, instead of making a flat pavlova, tower the edges and make more of an indent toward the middle to fill later with your topping.

Place the pavlova in the 300°F oven, and immediately drop the temperature to 225°F. Bake the pavlova for 80–90 minutes until

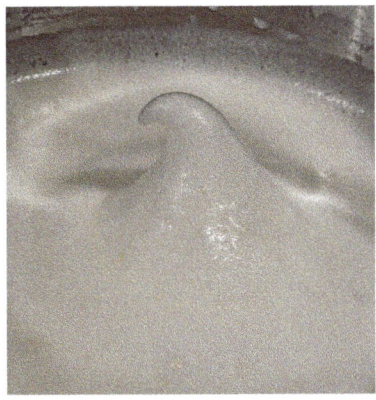

Egg whites whipped to soft peaks

Egg whites whipped to stiff peaks

Pavlova with a flat top spread onto pan ready to bake

the outside looks dry. Do not open the oven while the pavlova is baking, or it will collapse. When the pavlova is done baking, do not open the oven. Simply turn it off, and allow the pavlova to cool in the oven. You can take the pavlova out of the oven when the oven is cool. For me, this takes about 6 hours. The pavlova will collapse if you take it out early.

Once the oven is cool, your pavlova is ready to garnish and serve however you'd like. My favorite toppings are whipped cream and lemon curd.

Enjoy your pavlova!

Pavlova when done baking

Ladyfingers

Ingredients:

3 eggs, separated
1/2 c. sugar, divided
1/2 tsp vanilla
1/4 tsp salt
1 c. all-purpose flour
2 Tbsp cornstarch

BAKE 350°F
Bake: 12 minutes
Yield: 25 cookies
Ladyfingers are the base of a tiramisu.
Ladyfingers are not meant to be eaten alone. They are traditionally used as an element of another dessert.
Ladyfingers are very easy to make.

Preheat the oven to 350°F.

First, we need to separate the 3 eggs, placing the whites in a medium-sized bowl and the yolks in a second medium-sized bowl.

Whip the egg whites on medium speed until they reach soft peaks. You will know you have reached soft peaks when you can pick up the beaters and the peaks of egg whites bend over.

With the mixer running, add 1/4 cup of the sugar in a steady stream or add the sugar in 3 portions, mixing between each addition. Once all the sugar is added, continue mixing on high speed until you reach stiff peaks. You will know you have reached stiff peaks when you can pick the beaters up and the peaks of egg whites stand straight. Set aside.

Add the egg yolks to the remaining 1/4 cup sugar, along with the vanilla and salt, and beat on high speed until the mixture is thick and a pale yellow.

Once you are done beating the egg yolk mixture, pour it over the egg whites and fold to combine. Then sift the flour and cornstarch into the bowl, and fold to combine.

Once the batter is finished, transfer it to a piping bag or a gallon plastic zipper bag. If you would like, you can fit the piping bag with a 1/2-inch piping tip, but this is optional.

Line 2 baking sheets with parchment paper.

Snip the tip of your piping bag off so that you get a 1/2-inch nozzle. Onto the baking sheet, pipe cookies that are about 3 to 3 1/2 inches long and about 3/4-inch to 1-inch wide. Space them 1 to 2 inches apart. Once the cookies are piped, if you would like, you can dust them with powdered sugar.

Egg whites whipped to soft peaks

Egg whites whipped to stiff peaks

Egg yolks, sugar, vanilla, and salt beaten until thick and a pale yellow

Place the baking sheets into the oven, and bake for 12 minutes, until they are a pale golden brown. Transfer to a cooling rack to cool.

Enjoy your ladyfingers!

Piped ladyfingers

Ladyfingers when done baking

Tiramisu

Ingredients:

Ladyfingers:
3 eggs, separated
1/2 c. sugar, divided
1/2 tsp vanilla
1/4 tsp salt
1 c. all-purpose flour
2 Tbsp cornstarch

Tiramisu:
4 egg yolks
1/2 c. sugar, divided
1 1/2 c. whipping cream
1 tsp vanilla
8 oz. mascarpone
25 ladyfingers
1 1/2 c. espresso
(made from powdered
espresso)
Cocoa powder to dust

BAKE LADYFINGERS AT 350°F
Bake ladyfingers: 12 minutes
Yield: 9-inch square dish
*You will need powdered espresso
for this recipe. You cannot
substitute instant coffee.*
*This tiramisu has a wonderfully
creamy and smooth filling that
sets up well.*
*Tiramisu needs to set up in the
fridge for at least 4 hours.*
*Ladyfingers are the base of a
tiramisu.*

Preheat the oven to 350°F.

First we need to separate the 3 eggs, placing the whites in a medium-sized bowl and the yolks in a second medium-sized bowl.

Whip the egg whites on medium speed until they reach soft peaks. You will know you have reached soft peaks when you can pick up the beaters and the peaks of egg whites bend over.

With the mixer running, add 1/4 cup the sugar in a steady stream or add the sugar in 3 portions, mixing between each addition. Once all the sugar is added, continue mixing on high speed until you reach stiff peaks. You will know you have reached stiff peaks when you can pick the beaters up and the peaks of egg whites stand straight. Set aside.

Add the egg yolks to the remaining 1/4 cup sugar, along with the vanilla and salt, and beat on high speed until the mixture is thick and a pale yellow.

Once you are done beating the egg yolk mixture, pour it over the egg whites and fold to combine. Then sift the flour and cornstarch into the bowl, and fold to combine.

Once the batter is finished, transfer it to a piping bag or a gallon plastic zipper bag. If you would like, you can fit the piping bag with a 1/2-inch piping tip, but this is optional.

Line 2 baking sheets with parchment paper.

Snip the tip of your piping bag off so that you get a 1/2-inch nozzle. Onto the baking sheet, pipe cookies that are about 3 to 3 1/2 inches long and about 3/4-inch to 1-inch wide. Space them 1 to 2 inches apart. Once the cookies are piped, if you would like, you can dust them with powdered sugar.

Egg whites whipped to soft peaks

Egg whites whipped to stiff peaks

Egg yolks, sugar, vanilla, and salt beaten until thick and a pale yellow

Piped ladyfingers

Place the baking sheets into the oven and bake for 12 minutes, until they are a pale golden brown. Transfer to a cooling rack to cool. The cookies will cool very quickly.

While the cookies are cooling, let's get started on the tiramisu filling.

Place the egg yolks and 1/4 cup of the sugar into a medium-sized bowl, and whisk together. Place the bowl over a pot of water that is 1 inch deep, but do not let the bottom of the bowl touch the water. Turn the heat to medium-high. Heat the mixture until it reaches 140°F and all the sugar is dissolved.

Transfer the mixture to another bowl, cover it with plastic, and place in the freezer to cool it slightly while we get the rest of the tiramisu going.

Next, into the bowl of a stand mixer, place the whipping cream, 1/4 cup of sugar, and the vanilla. Whip until it is spreadable and reaches the consistency of whipped cream.

Add the mascarpone, and continue whipping until the mascarpone is mixed in.

Pour the egg yolk mixture over the whipped cream mixture, and whip the mixture until it is combined. Now the filling is ready!

Next, let's prepare the espresso. Mix together the espresso powder and water according to the instructions on the container. Pour it into a bowl just big enough to contain the liquid.

Then, set out an 8-inch or 9-inch square dish. Now let's dip the ladyfingers in the espresso.

Ladyfingers when done baking

Taking one ladyfinger at a time, quickly dip it in the espresso making sure to fully submerge it, but do not soak it in the liquid for any amount of time. Ladyfingers will get soft and break apart very fast, so dip them relatively quickly, but not so fast that they don't absorb any liquid.

Line the entire bottom of the dish with the ladyfingers. If you have gaps you need to fill in, break one of the cookies in half to fill in the gap.

Once the bottom of the dish is lined with ladyfingers, spread half of the filling over them. Then place another layer of dipped ladyfingers on top of the filling.

Finally, spread the rest of the filling on top.

To finish the tiramisu, dust the top with cocoa powder. An easy way to sprinkle the cocoa powder evenly is to place the cocoa powder into a small sifter and sprinkle it over the top.

Place the tiramisu in the fridge for at least 4 hours to set up.

Enjoy your tiramisu!

Chocolate Brownies

Ingredients:

8 Tbsp butter
1 1/2 c. sugar
1/2 c. cocoa powder
2 eggs
1 tsp vanilla
3/4 c. flour
1/2 tsp baking powder
1/4 tsp salt
2 Tbsp milk

BAKE 350°F
Bake: 28-35 minutes
Yield: 9-inch square dish
These brownies are wonderfully moist, fudgy, and flavorful. Brownies are easy to make.

Preheat the oven to 350°F, and grease an 8-inch or 9-inch square glass dish.

Place the butter in a medium-sized microwave-safe bowl. Microwave the butter until it is fully melted. Once melted, immediately add the sugar and mix until all the sugar is moistened. Add the cocoa powder, and continue to mix until it is fully combined.

Add the eggs and vanilla, and mix until just combined.

In a separate bowl, mix together the flour, baking powder, and salt. Once combined, add the flour mixture to the chocolate mixture and mix until mostly combined. Finally, add the milk to the brownie batter and mix until just combined.

Pour the brownie batter into the prepared dish, using a spatula to spread the batter evenly.

Bake the brownies for 35 minutes, until a toothpick inserted 2 inches from the edge of the pan comes out clean. Let the brownies cool on a wire cooling rack.

Enjoy your chocolate brownies!

The melted butter and the sugar mixed together

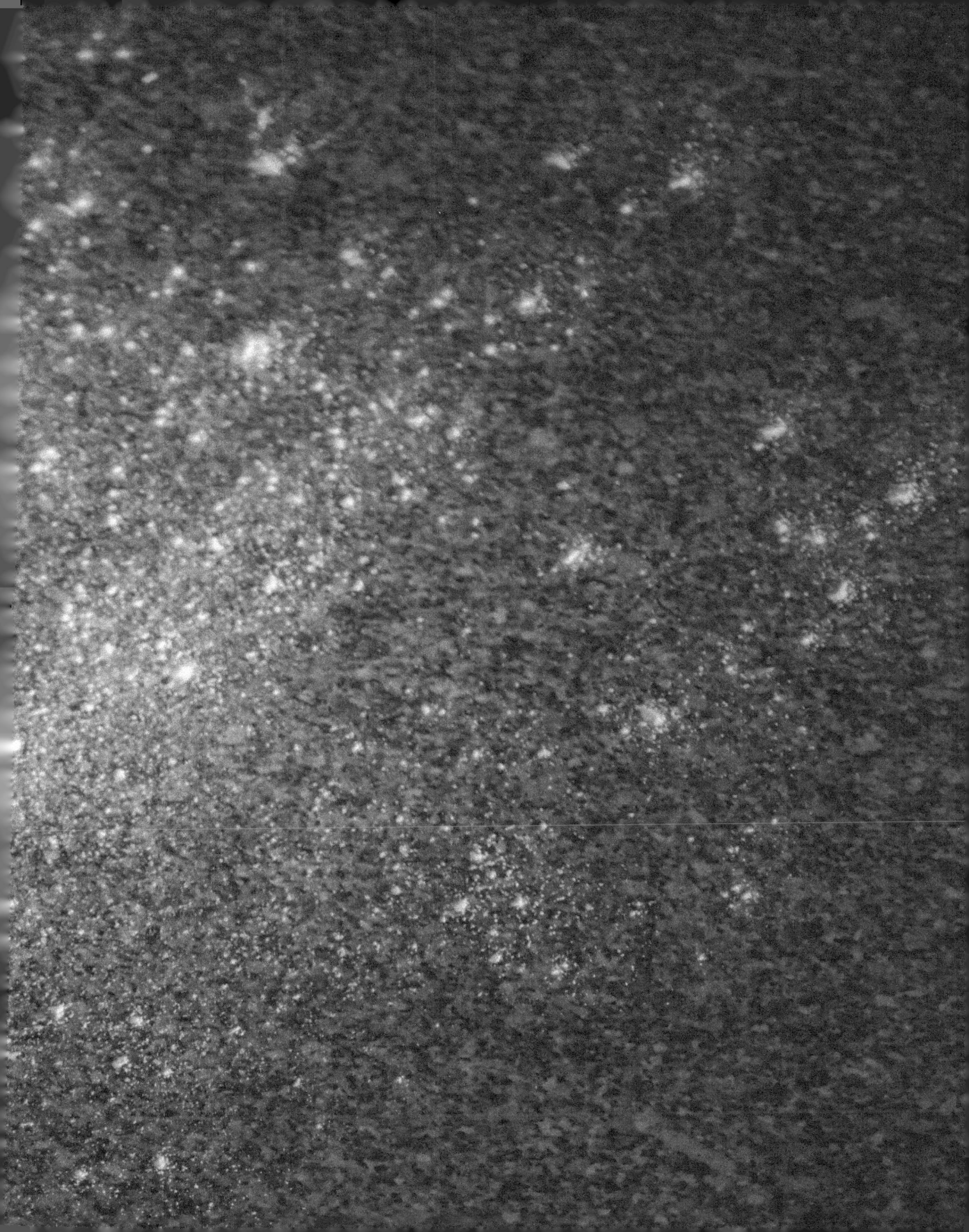